Praise for Dave Dictor & *MDC: Mem(*

"Long before 'Cop Killer' and 'Straight Ou_____ ...MDC. Hands down one of the most controversial, h_____...us in Hardcore, or...well...EVER. No one was neutral – least of ___ ...ie police. For those who might take for granted there was always this underground Punk Scene, with places to play in every town, this is a must read. What it really took to build your scene, and the sheer guts of the people who laid their asses on the line, this should be a real eye-opener." — Jello Biafra

"Dave Dictor taught me everything I know about balls, humility, getting through borders with a van full of dirty punks, and introducing the support act. On tour in Europe, kids yelled in the mic every word about loving chickens or hating John Wayne, and his dominatrix girlfriend joined Tribe 8 onstage, getting us banned in Hamburg by German feminists. MDC went to countries no other band would dare, risking arrest in order to bring real revolution to the truly oppressed. He has always searched out the outsiders in a scene of outsiders. Dave Dictor doesn't just sing punk, he lives it. This is his saga."
— Lynn Breedlove, Tribe 8

"Dave Dictor is somebody you can really count on. He is that rare breed that has not wavered over time, he has stuck to his beliefs, the kind of person that's out to make a better world." — Joe Shithead Keithley, DOA

"I knew Dave Dictor, the singer from MDC, and I used to crash in his room when he was on tour. The place was called the Rathouse. Everyone had a fanzine, everyone was in a band. My parents were either very brave or very stupid for letting me hang out with all these interesting, sexually diverse, drug-happy people." — Tre Cool, Green Day

"1982's *Millions of Dead Cops* album represented a milestone in radical politics and music. If Jello Biafra was hardcore's fiery Abbie Hoffman, MDC's Dave Dictor served as its cross-dressing Che Guevara."
— Steven Blush, *American Hardcore*

"When I first met Dave, there was an immediate recognition of a lifetime friendship. No matter if we were punk rock singers or cowboys on the range ... that friendship would have been there, is there. I love the guy."
— Gary Floyd, The Dicks / Sister Double Happiness / Black Kali Ma

"Dave Dictor was one of most furious, provocative and important front men in the original hardcore scene. He called his band 'Millions of Dead Cops,' and had the intelligence and fearlessness to back it up."

— Vic Bondi, Articles of Faith

"A pioneer in championing gay rights in the early days of punk, Dave has always been on the cutting edge of relevant issues and to this day he continues to inspire punk fans young and old. Essential reading for any punk enthusiast."

— Kieran Plunkett, The Restarts

"Dave MDC is a force multiplier. It is the bridge builders that help the scene and our communities, actively countering infighting, divisiveness, and injustice, not to mention just plain mean people being bullies. In a time when 'political' hardcore bands weren't very trendy at all, and 'punker-than-thou' was a tiresome poser pastime, he helped thousands of us punks and misfits navigate the punk scene, slam dancing, stage diving, and joyfully overriding junkie nihilism and the neo-Nazi skinhead movement with hard hitting conscious lyrics and dealing with shit that matters. The 1982 MDC album was a huge milestone. Everything in my life is divided into either before that fateful day I first picked it up (at the Ratcage record store in NYC's Lower East Side) and afterwards. Because of that record, I was able to connect with him and ended up touring with him on our Rock Against Reagan tour. Dave introduced us to the Dicks, the Crucifucks, Dead Kennedys, and Dirty Rotten Imbeciles (DRI), all of whom either toured with us or played at our shows throughout 48 states of the USA." — Alan "audiogrouch" Thompson, sound engineer, co-producer of Rock Against Racism NYC & Rock Against Reagan

MDC:
Memoir from a Damaged Civilization

also by Dave Dictor

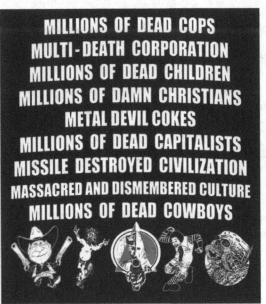

MILLIONS OF DEAD COPS
MULTI-DEATH CORPORATION
MILLIONS OF DEAD CHILDREN
MILLIONS OF DAMN CHRISTIANS
METAL DEVIL COKES
MILLIONS OF DEAD CAPITALISTS
MISSILE DESTROYED CIVILIZATION
MASSACRED AND DISMEMBERED CULTURE
MILLIONS OF DEAD COWBOYS

MDC

Memoir from a
Damaged Civilization

Stories of Punk, Fear, and Redemption

Dave Dictor

with photographs & tour documentation
from the archives of
Ron Posner

Manic D Press
San Francisco

★ unplug bush ★ destroy amerikkka ★

Disclaimer: This book is a memoir, a narrative composed from memories of personal experiences as best as I can remember them. Apologies if you remember things differently or if I've gotten names, dates, places, or anything else wrong. I wasn't taking notes at the time.

The publisher would like to thank Ron Posner and David Ensminger for their assistance in producing this book.

cover photo: Ed Colver   original cover design: Craig Williams

Cataloging in Publication data in available from the Library of Congress
ISBN 978-1-933149-98-1   Printed in Canada

For
Tammy Lundy and all the lineups of MDC including
Ron Posner, Al "Alschvitz" Schultz, Franco Mares,
Mikey Donaldson, Gordon Fraser, Eric Calhoun,
Bill Collins, Matt Freeman, Chris Wilder, Erica Liss,
Joe Strum, Roby Williams, Tom Roberts, Matt Van Cura,
Brendon Bekowies, Al "Albatross" Basin, David Hahn,
John Soldo, Mike Pride, Mike Smith, Jesse Cobb,
Russ Kalita, Felix Griffin, and Dejan Podobnik

And for people everywhere
struggling to be themselves

CONTENTS

26 Friday
CRIME
WOLVARINES
REPORTERs 10:30pm

DOORWAYS
DANCE THEATRE presents
BAR WARS BALLET FRI. SAT. 9:30pm

27 saturday
S.F. PHOTO BOOK BENEFIT
HYMINGSTEIN Formerly FRANK HYMING
ALIENATION
THE JARS
VARVE 10:30 P.M.

28 sunday
AUTHORITIES
WHIPPETTS
CoUNTeRPARTs
THE RANGErS 10:30P.M.

29 Monday
ALGO
BIG BOYS From TEXAS
WHITE SILENCE
DADDY X 10:30 P.M.

30 Tuesday
PENiS EnVY
RED ASPHALT
Patricia HURTs
IRONICS 10:30PM

1 WEDNESDAY
UPTIGHTS
BOX
GHOULs
N.K.G. 10:30PM

2 thursday
DEAD KENNEDYS
STAINS from TEXAS
THE DICKS FROM TEXAS
$4.00 10:30pm

3 Friday
VKTMS
AGENT ORANGE From ORaNGE COUNTY
B TEam
BRAT from L.A. 10:30pm
DOORWAYS DANCE THEATER BAR WARS 9:00 P.M.

4 saturday
VKTMS
TSOL from L.A.
Sic PLEAsuRE
UNDEAD 10:30 PM
Outrageous Beauty
Pageant ACTIVELY
9:00 pm

FAB MAB
443 BROADWAY SAN FRANCISCO 956-3315

Photo VKTMS
by TERA COFFER

DIRKSEN-MILLER PRODUCTIONS
1966 CALIFORNIA STREET · SUITE 8
SAN FRANCISCO, CALIFORNIA 94109
USA

NEW WAVE ROTTEN
RECORD CHART
& ROCK THEATRE PROGRAM
JUNE 26 thru 4 JULY

NO. 150

DIRKSEN-MILLER PRODUCTIONS DESIGN / ARTIST: ROGER I REYES PASTE-UP: D G Warren   © copyright 1981 Dirksen Miller Productions

We pulled up on the bawdy street of Broadway, where all the Gold Rush saloons once featured dance hall girls and rowdy discontents, and stepped out of the van into a bristling throng of 500 punks: a sea of studded leather and spiky haircuts. We stood, flabbergasted, taking it all in. The band that would become known as MDC had just driven from Austin, Texas, straight through to San Francisco, California, arriving at the Mabuhay Gardens on July 2, 1981.

Inside, taking the stage, we began strumming our first song with all those eyes nailed to us as if we were in the Roman Coliseum. Everybody was ready to make the thumbs up or thumbs down. We rocked through "Business on Parade," and as we played "Dead Cops," the crowd grew feverish. By the third song, we had the crowd, and we just blew through our punk, hardcore, thrash set dressed in our street cowboy, blue denim, Goodwill outfits.

It was beyond anything we had ever experienced. I recall smiling at Ron as we realized these people got us, really understood what we had practiced and executed 500 times before. By the time we did "John Wayne Was A Nazi," our last song (we had a lean, 14-song set of short songs), the crowd just went bonkers.

We knew at that moment that this was our new home, and that the future was now.

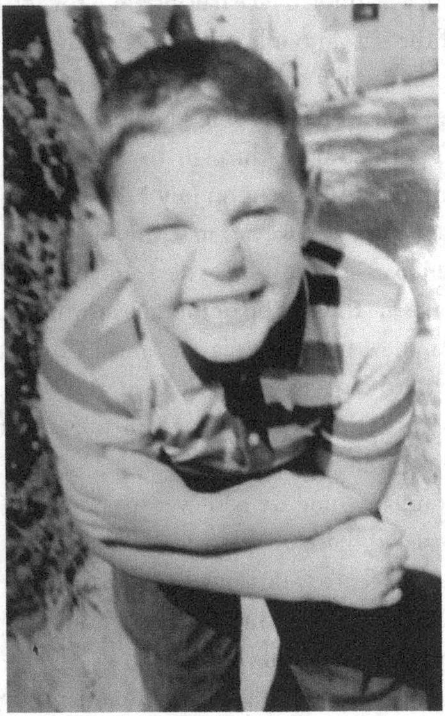

My Family Is A Little Weird

My first years on this planet, it seemed to me, I was very much on my own. My blood father, Teddy Dictor, was a private investigator and was frequently off somewhere trying to live like a character in a Raymond Chandler novel: nightclubbing, boating, and chatting up the dames.

As a reporter for the *New York Daily News*, back when the staff was chained to typewriters in the office, my mother was at work a lot, too, so I was deposited with various people. My grandmother lived down the hall from us. When I'd stay with her, I'd play with Tutti Frutti, the daughter of her friend. Tutti and I were mesmerized by each other and were left alone, a lot. We held hands and dug each other quite a bit. She was my first best friend in life and it was a beautiful thing. The fact that my first best friend was female influenced my close friendships with women, a reality that has lasted throughout my life to this day.

In the apartment building where we lived was a tall black-haired woman who lived upstairs. She was mysterious and walked past with an elegant Natalie Wood-like flair. When I saw her coming, I'd run to the front door, open it for her, and she'd say, "Well, thank you, my dear young man."

It was 1960, and my 5-year-old head would swim between the sight, sound, and scent of this woman. My heart would flutter. As she passed, Chanel No. 5 lingering in her wake, I got plain ol' excited, and those were my first erections in life. I didn't understand it and certainly couldn't control it, but there it was... I was having questionable sexual feelings at the tender age of five.

My brother was five years older than me. He had already started school when my parents split up, and he took their break-up a lot harder than I did. I was only two when my mom divorced my blood father, Teddy, who subsequently moved to Florida, rarely to be heard from or seen thereafter. He was Jewish; my mom was Catholic. Intermarriage was not common or accepted in the 1940s or '50s. The Jewish branch of our family never really accepted us; and the Italian Catholic branch looked at me with a jaundiced eye. This feeling of being an outsider from an early age, though I did not really understand it at the time, also deepened my sensitivity of how it feels to not fit in.

As a kid, I went to two very small Catholic schools. One was Presentation Boys School and the other was St. Boniface. Having something to believe in, my mother reasoned, might mitigate the negative effects of being left alone to my devices much of the time. I really bought into it all. I tried to become an altar boy year after year. I had to memorize long psalms, and I kept getting rejected by the powers that be. I went to Catholic camps in the summer, and I thought everyone in the world was Catholic.

Sister Marybeth was my first grade teacher. I asked her about the difference between boys and girls. She told me we were all the same, but girls were inside out. I was quite taken with her answer. It made so much sense to me... Humphrey Bogart and Lauren Bacall, Franklin and Eleanor Roosevelt, and Elvis Presley and Ann Margaret were all really the same. This idea, more than anything, shaped my view of gender roles having no clear dividing lines.

When I was age seven, President John Kennedy was shot. I felt that something more than terrible had happened: something truly sinister was going on behind the curtains. Still, I prayed in earnest, hoping for some answers. I didn't get them. I was a disillusioned nine-year-old and already a recovering Catholic. A few years later, Martin Luther King and Robert Kennedy were also murdered. By then, I was a flat out cynical tween.

When I turned nine, we moved from Jamaica, Queens, to Sea Cliff, Long Island, and I went to a different Catholic school. Then two years later, we moved again, this time to Glen Cove, the neighboring town. I was eleven and went to public middle school for the first time, where the kids were much more socially advanced than I was. I was out of my league. When I confidently told my classmates at this new school that I was pretty sure Santa Claus existed, they answered back, in no uncertain terms, "There is... NO... Santa Claus. We're absolutely sure." I was shocked. It was a big school. All of a sudden, there were kids from different backgrounds. Some of the Jewish kids were dating already. After moving around and switching schools a few times, I was a bit lost.

Earlier, after she quit her job at the paper, my mom and the person who would become the man who raised me, Joseph Hanlon, started an automobile transporter business. My mother did the books and worked dispatch. Later, my mom married Joe, whom I considered to be my father more than my blood father. He had five sons from a previous marriage, so there we were: two parents and seven sons all in a big house in Glen Cove. I was in the middle, with four older brothers and two younger brothers. Everyone treated me well. Eventually, I made friends in the new neighborhood and made my way around.

In sixth grade, I made my first lifelong best friend. Mark Dubicki and I sat next to each other in class and hung out with each other like glue that year and most of the next forty-five. I must admit we lost contact occasionally for years at a time, but we were always best friends. I was like Rocky to his Bullwinkle, Mutt to his Jeff. He was bigger than me, tougher, a man's man, whereas I had a tad more common sense.

Another one of my new friends, Gail B., and I were in a slew of classes together in seventh grade. She was among my first crushes. I don't how it started; I just remember us both looking over at each other in the classroom and eventually smiling back and forth. We would meet up after school on our 20" frame bicycles with banana seats, and we would ride and climb trees and head out to the beach to skim rocks. She was the ultimate tomboy who could bike as fast as me and climb trees better. We would lie in the grass and talk about every concern of our young minds. Sometimes we would wrestle each other.

One time, when I had her pinned, I drooled into her mouth to mess with her. She reacted hard and fast by flipping me over and jamming a clump of earth-caked sod into my mouth. I gagged, laughed, and spat up dirt as she started laughing. We sat looking at each other, eventually hugging and pecking each other with kisses. This was the easiest and sweetest part of my childhood. In the evenings, we would talk to each other on the phone for hours the way teens do. When school let out for summer break that year, I got a call from Gail. She told me she was moving, and a few days later it happened: she was gone. We were two peas in a pod and then... we weren't.

Then when I was in 8th grade, there were these hard-ass dudes — we used to call them "hoods" — from the Nassau Boys gang. These guys used to terrorize my hometown. Most of these guys are dead, lifetime prison dudes, some made it out, but they were tough nuts for teenagers, like the Sharks in *West Side Story*, except none of them danced in sync. Anyway, they wanted to recruit my best friend, Mark, so they came onto the junior high playground at lunchtime.

These hard cases just about never went to school. They were big on huffing glue, getting in rumbles, and doing time at juvenile lockup. Anyway, one day, they showed up and surrounded Mark. The recess bell rang, and everybody, fearing for themselves, ran inside. I stayed outside and watched from about fifteen yards off. They took turns slapping Mark, trying to egg him into a fight, so they all could jump him at the same time. And what they really wanted was for Mark to take a beating then join their gang. He refused. They slapped him, told him to cry, which he either wouldn't, or couldn't, do. Mark had this big, strong brother, five years his elder, and he taught Mark how to take a slap and not cry.

This was way over me. I was scared shitless. I would have cried, begged, and tap-danced. Mark was scared, but he just wouldn't cry, blow after blow. They noticed me, but didn't pay me much mind. I wasn't the tough they were looking for. In fact, I was anti-tough, yet they noticed I hadn't split on Mark. They finally got afraid some authorities were going to check it out and call the police so they took off.

Mark reminded me of this story a while ago, telling me, "Homeboy, that's why I'd never abandon you." And even though Mark and I were not classic jocks or scholastically-inclined, we became revered in this special kind of way because we were known to be loyal friends.

That same year in junior high school, Mark and I put on a wrestling exhibition for our class Gym Night with hundreds of our classmates and their parents in attendance. Many classmates performed stuff like climbing up the ropes and shooting foul shots, and the girls did gymnastics and cheerleader routines. Real dullsville, you can imagine.

Mark and I decided to do a fake wrestling match. We were supposed to do the standard Roman-Greco high school wrestling thing, but we were gonna blow that off and do the fake punch, kick, slap, poor man's version of the WWF, but at the last second, I blew it and started traditional wrestling. Neither of us had worn jock straps for the occasion, so when we started really going for it, well, it got interesting for the three minutes or so it lasted.

From the beginning, people howled and hooted, and then all of a sudden everyone broke out in laughter. I mean, roaring laughter. Finally, the gym teacher understood. We didn't, for we thought we were just being naturally good showmen. Mr. Lamberson blew his whistle long and hard.

After that night and into the next day, we got the idea. All the girls we went to school with said things like, "Thanks for the exhibition, guys, you really showed your stuff," and "Way to go, Mark and Dave, stealing the show, fellas." We finally got it. Our genitalia were hanging out for all to see. Needless to say, all those girls started dating older guys, and we were quite left in the dust. "Way to go!" Yeah, right.

One night around that same time, when I was 12 or 13, I was sitting at home watching the evening news. There was John Wayne on television, giving a speech at a pro Vietnam War rally in Cambridge, Massachusetts, home of Harvard. The Duke, standing on a tank, wanted America to turn the tank's cannons on anti-war protesters. I was brought up on John Wayne movies. All of a sudden, I had to make a choice: were his political views okay? No, they were not. He made me sick to my stomach. I realized a lot of the propaganda we were fed was just that: propaganda.

By the time I was 16, I became a radicalized high school student. With the Vietnam War ongoing in the background, the shootings at Kent State in May 1970, which prompted my whole high school class to walk out of school, and all the protests against Richard Nixon as president, being an anti-system teen was almost easy.

Along the way, I picked up a fondness for wearing women's undergarments. I started noticing this predilection in fifth or sixth grade while looking at women's underwear advertisements in the Sunday newspaper. Shoot, I'd get raging erections just thinking about them (doesn't everybody?). I had no one to share this with, so I felt alone. I have always been attracted to females. A lot of folks even now think, "If you wear women's clothing, you must be gay." I have a transvestism fetish, but in my case, I have not yet been physically attracted to men, though I've always been open about my sense of gender fluidity. Who knows what the future will bring? There are so many ways of loving. I realized early on my sexuality didn't fall into the "normal" category. I stood with sexual outlaws such as David Bowie, Lou Reed, and Ray Davies, who were heroes in my early teens.

The MDC song, "My Family Is A Little Weird," was written when I was 16, a pretty young age, years before punk, with the same basic chords but played in a slow country style.

The song's origins came from an event at Glen Cove High School that had the senior girls playing the junior girls in a basketball game, while certain boys signed up to dress and act like cheerleaders. My virginity taker, Patty, really femmed me up. I was the cheerleading star for my junior year homies. The year was 1972, and I was taking "a walk on the wild side," or so it seemed to me. The older jock guys in the senior class hated it because this confirmed that I was not straight, not one of them. They were acting like Biff and his bully buddies in *Back To The Future*. They swore that I'd be getting mine soon, and they lived up to that promise the following week by fattening my lip and blackening my eye. Anyway, that was the night I wrote "My Family Is A Little Weird."

MY FAMILY IS A LITTLE WEIRD

My family is a little weird
Daddy wears a dress, Mommy grows a beard
All our neighbors complain all the time
Really don't understand my kind
Little brother was thrown out of school
Drownin' kiddies in the kiddie pool
Big brother lives in city jail
Mom and Dad won't pay his bail
Big sister complains all the time
She's hooked on barbs and wine
All my aunts are lying whores
All my uncles are drinking bores
Grandma sells dope to high school kids
Grandpa don't care, his mind's on the skids
No one seems to understand
Not sure if I'm a woman or a man

"My family" was a metaphor: *I* was a little weird.

Fast-forward to the 1980s, as the scene shifted from arty, free-for-all punk to a more testosterone-driven, male-oriented hardcore, a lot of bands had members who didn't understand about being different and who hadn't been exposed to much diversity.

American hardcore, with its macho stances, seemed to need a queer person to stand up for differences among punks. I went along with that idea by giving ambiguous answers in interviews, like when people were curious about the MDC song on our first album, "America's So Straight."

A typical question: "Are you gay?"

My reply: "Doesn't everyone have some gay feelings now and then?"

19

When offered my first joint at 13 in 1969, I took it and inhaled. I felt, *What the fuck?* like I wanted to "Kiss the sky..." as Jimi Hendrix sang. Soon, I was drinking, trying acid, Quaaludes, and black beauties.

One day, a guy phoned my friend Patty's house by mistake. Instead of slamming the phone down ("Wrong number!"), she flirted with the stranger, so he brought over a pound of pot and some Orange Sunshine acid, which led to months of edgy teenage kicks.

He fronted it all to us. At 14, Mark and I were dealing to students much older than us. We were holding the bag, and, on top of that, Mark's mother didn't have a true sense of right and wrong, so she was in on it. She drove us to our deals and took us on vacations that were paid for with drug money. We went to Disney World, Hershey Park, Lake Champlain, and everywhere else we wanted to go.

Mark's family was nothing like mine. Besides driving Mark and me around on our drug deals, Mrs. Dubicki would also take us to go shoplifting at major department stores. This was before all the high tech surveillance and special tags. We made out just like bandits, stoned bunnies the whole way. She'd also call the school, claim she was my mother, and state that I would be out sick for a week, and we'd go on a trip to Florida, or to Hershey, Pennsylvania, to a Grateful Dead concert, and, quite often, just for a relaxing day at the beach.

I am amazed we made it through school. I was absent a lot but managed to get straight C's. When I did muster the will to go to school, our social studies teacher, Mr. Claybourne, who was gay, would get stoned with us, including once in the classroom with about ten of us students, and many other nights over at his apartment. These were the early '70s, and it was Fast Times at Glen Cove High. While I'm at it, let me mention Mark stood up for me, next to me, time after time against older jocks, crazy psychos, and other assorted macho/violence-oriented moments of my youth.

Sometime along the way, Patty took me to bed. When I confessed I'd like to wear a pair of her panties, she enthusiastically obliged. It was a nice way to lose my virginity. Thank you very much, Patty. Just remember, as the Beatles sang, "Everybody's got something to hide, except for me and my monkey."

Music, to a lot of us, then and now, was the soundtrack to, and a very big part of, our lives. My mom bought me my first Beatles record at age seven. "I Wanna Hold Your Hand" and the B-side, "She Loves You," were great. The Beatles released records that seemed to get better and better every year. In later years, younger band members tried to tell me Metallica was greater than the Beatles. Not in my book. Anyway, my 45-rpm collection meant everything to me. AM radio was king growing up, and there was a lot of great music on there. I always related to the Jackson Five, The Four Tops, and Little Stevie Wonder.

At 12, I was into The Monkees and Otis Redding's song, "Sitting on the Dock of the Bay." At 13, my older brothers introduced me to the Grateful Dead, Cream, the Yardbirds, and Janis Joplin. My mother turned me on to Arlo Guthrie and took me to see the movie, "Alice's Restaurant" in real time. The dream of being a musical artist was ever-present in my mind.

I started talking to my mother about vegetarianism because I questioned why we were eating animals. She bought me an Epiphone guitar and suggested I write a song about it. She encouraged me to play my own songs, and start working to change the world. Thank you very much, Mom. I was not alone, and my circle of friends all started picking up instruments. This was still way before punk rock.

When I was 15, the basement of Claudia's, a women's dress shop in my hometown of Glen Cove, Long Island, was a Mafia poker room, complete with working women. One time, I went with a friend at night. I had $23 to my name, probably left over from birthday money. They let me in, and directed me to the back room where the prostitutes worked. Dirty Gertie chose me and took me into one of the stalls. I was $7 short on the transaction, but that didn't seem to matter. She asked what I would like to do. I asked if I could lick her. She laughed, pushed my head down to her crotch, and told me I was her "dick for brains," which became the MDC song "Dick For Brains" on our first album.

DICK FOR BRAINS

Oh Goddess, I love you, it's true
I'll do anything you want me to
Why? Why?
Dick for brains, dick for brains
Why am I your dick for brains?
You know it drives me so insane

You know I love your power
I wait on your golden shower
Why? Why?
Dick for brains, dick for brains

Not a woman with a clit for brains
You know it drives me so insane
You know how I try to please
Got carpet burns on my knees
Why? Why?
Why? Why?
Dick for brains, dick for brains
Why am I your dick for brains?
You know it drives me so insane

I love it when you treat me cruel
Let me have the whole damn rule
Why? Why?
Dick for brains, dick for brains
Why am I your dick for brains?
You know it drives me so insane

My first band was called The Covers, as in "from Glen Cove." We jammed, mostly on Bob Dylan, Reverend Gary Davis, and traditional bluegrass covers. We gigged at the beach for small gatherings and at the homes of each band member. I learned how to crunch those chords in front of friendly faces. We also started hitting the road to nearby New York City, where we absorbed loud live music, concerts including Humble Pie, Jeff Beck, the Winter Brothers, Hot Tuna, and many others.

By the time we were seniors in high school, life was really... just easy. I started to wonder, *What comes next? What are my dreams?* I desired to travel and see the world with a guitar at the ready, but that was about it. My mother pleaded for me to try a little college since I would be the first person in her family to go to college, and hopefully graduate. I felt obliged to go along with this but I left the application process and choice of college up to her.

After our last day of high school, Mark and I skipped graduation and drove the Trans Canada Trail together. We wound up cracking up our car in San Diego, then hitchhiked back across the country, both of us 17 years old.

That fall, in 1973, I started college at a small school named Hartwick College in upstate Oneonta, NY. I ended up that winter at the staid, conservative University of Tampa in Florida where I met my future drummer, Al Schultz. We were both New Yorkers and both enjoyed recreational drugs Al had a near encyclopedic mind when it came to all things musical. He played a Gene Krupa inspired style of drums, except as a lefty. His paradiddle drum strokes, even then, went from upside down to inside out and were way rocking and unique.

At school that freshman year, a friend of ours, Tate Bryant, broke into a drug store and stole a minor amount of pharmaceuticals on the way out the door. Police ordered him to stop. He kept going and was shot in the back, dead. He died for a few vials of drugs. It reinforced my distrust of law enforcement because I realized that the police can, and will, shoot you dead for a minor crime. This incident definitely played into the naming of our band seven years later.

That same year in Tampa, Al and I briefly met a good-looking girl named Jenny Jo Brown in a diner near the university. Jenny Jo and I were destined to meet again years later at the Vats in San Francisco, where I was living with the band. Crazy is this game of life with so many coincidences.

After spending freshman year in Tampa, I went back north and read how Boston University had great Creative Writing courses. I got accepted to BU, and with my parents' help, off to Boston I went. In those courses, people reacted positively toward my writing for the first time. It made me feel good and I found myself thrown into songwriting. People still weren't going crazy for my singing voice but I was gaining confidence.

I knew I could write.

Going Home with the Armadillo

I was still feeling restless. After two years of college, and a summer hanging with my high school bandmates, I rambled down to Austin, Texas in the fall of 1976 because I wanted in on some action and Boston wasn't doing it for me. Austin is, and was, a really great place, but back then it was a sleepy hippie college town that also happened to be the capital of Texas. It had this great country swing music scene. I was writing a lot of country songs and fancied myself as one who might just fit in there. I thought before long I'd be showing my songs off to Willie and Waylon and the boys. I got there and immediately got a job at Domino's as a pizza delivery driver making $3.50 an hour. It was enough to afford an $85-a-month room. Soon, I was out and about, trying to show off my stuff.

After several months of not having any luck trying to meet people who knew people, or figuring out a way to get to other people looking for songs, I always ended up in front of a Chicano bar named Raul's. They were hosting an open mike on Monday nights, and that was where I met folks who labeled themselves "punks." They were friendly and snide and anti-everything, which I liked, having come from a disappointed 1970s anti-war, anti-nuke, pro-pot, activist background.

Aptly, I wrote "I Hate Work" at my Domino's job, played it for my crew of Monday evening punks, and they loved it. Nobody had ever reacted to one of my songs like that: they were dancing and talking about what I should name my band. At that moment, it was like, screw straight-world music, *I! Am! A! Punk! Rocker!*

I HATE WORK

work work work it's a lot of jive
never gonna work 9 to 5
tell Mr. Bossman I said goodbye
never gonna work another day in my life

[chorus:]
I hate work, yeah I do
I hate work, and you should too
I hate work, ain't no clerk
I hate work, ain't no jerk

never gonna work in a factory
or sweat my life in misery
work like that never meant to be
work like that is not for me

[chorus]

work work work away the years of your life
work work work never see your wife
work work work sweat and tears
work work work lost my years

[chorus]

we're not gonna work in your crummy jobs
we're not gonna fight in your stinkin' wars
we're not gonna vote in your phony elections
take a good look we're your reflection

Once that musical decision was made, the spigot opened wide and a deluge of songs started to flow.

Since 1975, vegetarianism has been a tenet of my life. Since I loved cartoon animals, I thought I shouldn't eat them. That idea dawned on me in my early teens, so I gave up real animals: flesh, blood, and bone. I decided to start going meatless at 17. I asked my mother about it, and she said, "If that is how you feel, then do it."

She started making my dishes separate from everyone else's. Her support was crucial. She was an animal lover though not a vegetarian, yet still she was empathetic from the start. Upon leaving home at 19, I found the world a very different place. There was no Whole Foods at the time, and my incredibly thorough research led me to believe only Gandhi and Hitler had been vegetarians. So I figured that there were three of us.

In 1976, I wrote the song "Chicken Squawk" with my two dear buddies, Jim Brighton and Butch Zito, for our Glen Cove band, the Solar Pigs. I put the vegetarian edge to it with Jim's help.

CHICKEN SQUAWK

When I walk into the store
They sell the chickens by the score
But eating dead birds just ain't for me
I don't eat roast beef or fish
Porky Pig is not my dish
Just go ahead and let your chickens be
In chicken circles, it's Adolph Perdue
Wants to feed featherless chicken to you
I don't take orders from Colonel Sanders
Do you?
I don't wanna eat no hens
Not even every now or then
Wanna let all the chickens be

[chorus:]
Bawk, bawk, bawk...
Swing to the east and swing to the west
Swing with the chickens you love best
Come on down and do the chicken squawk with me

Wishing Daffy lots of luck
Cause Elmer Fudd's a-hunting duck
They're dreaming about their little fricassee
And Bugs Bunny is a friend of mine
Eating him I'd feel like Frankenstein
Eating flesh seems pretty foul to me
So on Thanksgiving or Christmas Eve
Give them turkeys a reprieve
Ain't no turkey got to die for me
Foghorn Leghorn wrote to me
Says MDC's alright by me
Cause we all learned to let our chickens free

[chorus]

Lordy Jesus this must be the end
They got us eating our cartoon friends
Emancipate those little chickadees
Swing to the east and swing to the west
Swing to the chicken you love best
Come and do the chicken squawk with me

By 1978, health food and organic veggie stores started popping up. Soon I realized I was not alone, and after meeting Ron Posner and Franco Mares, who were not only punk rockers but also vegetarians, too.

I gave "My Family Is A Little Weird" a punk makeover. With my three-song set that included "Chicken Squawk," I was happening.

However, a band name was still needed, as well as instruments, amps, cabinets, microphones, and a musical collaborator: all easier said than done. I wanted someone compatible who could include me in their vision, as well as them in mine. Well, along came Ron Posner, pedaling with some friends who were meeting up on bicycles at Barton Springs Creek. We started talking about being in a band, and he was just as excited as I was. He was an accomplished classical guitar player from Venezuela, but I was soon to learn he could play whole sides of many Who albums, and he was a thorough, intricate, double-stroking rhythm guitar player. We clicked right away, like within the first song or two. I knew I had my first partner, and we would create a punk band. It felt good. Really good.

Over the course of the next few months, we practiced at our homes, working on a three or four song set. We played out at maybe two or three house parties. Our first band was the Rejects with Ron's girlfriend, Amy, as lead singer, and then someone said, "Let's spell it Reejex." Then we morphed into the Stains, with me as the lead singer.

DAVE   FRANC'O   AL   RON

MILLIONS OF DEAD COPS

Ron is my best buddy who co-founded the band that would come to be known as MDC with me, and is a guitar ace who works at his craft ceaselessly. He truly knows, and takes to heart, the saying that the way to Carnegie Hall and success is to "practice, practice, practice," but he is also someone who is up on what is going on in this world, keeping well informed on issues of social and economic injustices. Ron and I made a conscious decision to distinguish ourselves as more politically-oriented than other bands around at the time.

Ron has been my co-vegetarian from the beginning. We're very different from each other, yet we have always complemented each other. He demands to practice a full week before any gig. "Good enough" is not good enough for him, and, man, I appreciate that. I can take too many short cuts, and he doesn't let me do that. He is a hardcore machine, while I am a punk. He demands his band to make full efforts, and this is why that first album is so killer. I am fortunate to have met him in the late 1970s when I did because, without him helping to create and shape the music to go along with my words, I wouldn't be writing this book today.

My friend, Mara Beth Israel Ubie, says you're lucky to have a few people who are true blue in your life. Ron is one of those few true blues. May all you good people be so lucky as to find true blues in your lives.

Bass player Franco Mares was my bandmate on and off for ten years. We met at a protest of Henry Kissinger's policies at the 1978 Republican Governors' Association Conference held in Austin, an event that included eight protesters and a thousand Republican operatives and players. All the Republican convention goers looked at us and laughed. We had signs that read, "Support Poverty, Vote Republican," and "Henry K, Go Away!"

The conventioneers toyed with us, but it was still terribly fun how we ribbed them as they did us. Jimmy Carter was president, and some hope was still alive. Franco and I hit it off from the start. Soon we formed an anti-nuclear group to go from Austin, TX to Seabrook, NH to protest the nuclear power plant there. These were my first political actions that went beyond signing a petition, collecting petitions, or holding a sign at a protest in previous years.

Once The Stains/MDC was up and running in Austin in 1981, Franco and I pushed each other to do benefits. We did the 1984 Peace Compilation with music from 52 bands worldwide. More than $10,000 from sales of the compilation went to British and American anti-nuke groups, to the African National Congress, to Tractors for Nicaragua, and some went to people whose bands played on the record who were fighting disease.

MDC played hundreds of benefits through the years, including Big Mountain on Navajo land in northern Arizona in 1988, and at Mercury, NV nuclear protests with Seeds of Peace in the late '80s. They ran a soup kitchen at protests for environmental causes all over the West, and we worked with them. MDC was also proud to be called by Keith McHenry, founder of Food Not Bombs, "their house band" in San Francisco.

Through the years, I have met so many good people fighting for human rights, animal rights, indigenous peoples' rights, hunger causes, political prisoners, social causes, computers for Sao Paulo youth center, and more. Many punk bands have taken up the fights for environmental and social justice, too, so bless them as well. Proudly, we advocated. Franco was there in spirit with me all the time. His last year of life he played acoustic hunger protests in front of the White House. He died in rural Mexico, December 2009, when he didn't get the proper antibiotics in time during a brief illness. He was a great spirit.

Drummer Al Schultz, also known as Alschvitz, was the first friend who would go on to be in MDC. Al was received professional musical training in Manhattan. In his early teens, he saw live performances including the classic Jimi Hendrix opening for The Monkees tour, and many more who solidified his musical passions. Al could talk your ear off about Ira Gershwin's "Rhapsody In Blue," all types of jazz, rare 1950s rock and roll, operas, everything.

His mother, Ruth, who was also my friend, was a Broadway actress with a great sense of humor. She knew Manhattan nightlife inside and out. Al came from New York show business types: vaudeville and the like. His heroes were Buddy Rich and Billy Cobham, so his inclination as our drummer was to speed everything up. That turned out to be perfect as we transformed from a punk band to a thrash unit in the very beginning of hardcore in early 1981. Al is brilliant and has a mind for puzzles: he can finish the *New York Times* Sunday crossword puzzle in two hours. Unfortunately, I willingly followed him down a path to hard drugs and hard delivery systems. It's easy to follow a friend you look upon as a genius down some dark avenues. He lives in Portland but isn't currently active with the band, maybe sometime in the future.

In the beginning, when Ron and I were starting the band, I met Tammy Lundy. Soon, we were hanging together day and night plotting to make the band better. She fell into the position of manager, but she was much more. For one thing, she did art. She helped me write a lot of the songs, listened to my words, and told me if I was going in the right direction. She helped me pen "No Place To Piss" and had a direct effect on many of my songs. I felt we were a co-ed unit.

Tammy let me know when my chauvinism bled into sexism. The sixties era I was raised in was full of sexism, both subtle and overt. Hardcore bands in the early eighties didn't have girls around. Girls were supposed to be girlfriends and were expected to stay at home.

The Bad Brains blatantly pronounced the weird anti-girl philosophy. We weren't having any of it. Females were an integral to our machine. And, heck, we always liked and respected women, and understood the revolution needed them.

Tammy was so cool, hung cool, and didn't play games. She traveled with the band from 1981 to 1984. She's always been a good person, a sweet person, and a politically aware person. She's currently a librarian for the city of San Francisco and regularly comes to our shows. She was crucial to the success of MDC and, for that, I will always be grateful.

Our friends, Anita Collison of the Bay Area and Lisa "Bat" Smith of Toronto, were also early additions to the MDC family, joining us on the road, doing that roadie work, designing fliers, pre-planning Rock Against Reagan ideas, and more. Thank you.

Mark Dubicki and I had moved to Austin, where we worked and lived together. When the Stains/MDC started to happen four or five years later, Mark was our on-again, off-again roadie. Working for MDC, he pulled me out of more dangerous situations than I can remember, involving assorted rednecks and hard-nosed skinheads and punks from coast to coast, until the late 1980s. He was very loyal, always there for me. And then, after one of those tours, Mark met someone, got married, and we lost touch for six or seven years.

One day, my mom called me up in Portland to say Mark's mother, Estelle, had died, and that Mark was at his parents' house. That is one of the few phone numbers forever etched onto my brain. He picked up the phone and said, "Hey, homeboy, where you been at?" and when I moved back to New York in the late '90s, we picked up the friendship. He lived right down the road with his wife and three kids, driving a train for the Philly subway line, and we got together a lot that winter.

Sadly, Mark Dubicki passed on in December 2013. Fucking lung cancer, two months from diagnosis until he died. Hug your loved ones, everybody.

I would be remiss if I did not salute the fabulous and dear Gary Floyd, without whom the Stains/MDC would not have existed. The

Stains were indebted to Gary's band, the Dicks. I met Gary and was so inspired that I let go of materialism and just trusted that I was here to sing songs of rebellion and live on the fringe. The Dicks were, and are, my favorite band of all time and symbolized Texas punk to a T.

Gary Floyd and Randy "Biscuit" Turner of the Big Boys personified punk and funk. I cannot stress enough the effect of Gary and Randy as movers and shakers of the Texas punk scene. They turned the scene from a few hundred artsy, late '70s, University of Texas Radio, Television, and Film major types into the multi-thousand-person, incredible Austin scene that created me, Felix Griffin of DRI, David Yow, the Offenders, and so many other performers and bands. Gary's sheer personality shaped the Texas scene just as Ian MacKaye's shaped the DC scene or Joey Shithead's shaped the Canadian scene, and on and on.

MDC toured with the Dicks to San Francisco in 1981, which launched us as a national band. Gary combined a radical working class consciousness with a razor sharp wit. Due to him, I was fortified and fierce about economic injustice and strengthened my resolve against homophobia, which did indeed run amuck back in the '80s. This allowed me to stand up to the Bad Brains and so many other bands that were homophobic on one level or another. I received so much from Gary. I love him dearly, forever.

On a semi-related note, I was talking to another good friend, Amyl, of the Spider Cunts and Imperial Leather. She showed me a facial scar she now wears across her cheek, and the gnarly picture of that 1" x 4" cut on her face taken in the emergency room. Some hardcore dude named Ducky from LA who is still out on the loose gave it to her. What was especially sad to her was that all these acquaintances, thought to be friends, saw it go down in the backyard of the punk house they were hanging at. Everybody just froze and didn't come through like you'd hope people are gonna do for you. People played neutral, didn't want to get involved, didn't stick up for her like she'd thought they would. Amyl and I agreed, that's what really counts in this life: people who stick by you and don't play it weak when the shit comes down.

Don't follow people blindly into hell... but if bad shit is going down, don't leave your friends high and dry. So that's the point: back up your friends in word and deed, in thick and thin, and not just when it's convenient. That's what friendship costs sometimes, but real friendships are one of the things that make life worth living. Let me repeat it: hug your loved ones today.

PUNK ROCK AGAINST THE KLAN AND POLICE BRUTALITY

DICKS
STAINS
DROOGS
VESTALS

duke's
april 3
fri.

benefit for
the John
Brown anti-
klan comm.

No War, No KKK, No Fascist USA

Austin is a beautiful place, but it's still in Texas, a state that is home to the infamous train song "Midnight Special" and where counties like King County are owned and run by one family. The Ku Klux Klan was active, and they infamously appeared in cop cars, sitting in the front seat and chatting up the police like they were one and the same. In Galveston, the Klan headquarters sat openly off the main highway like a post office.

In the late '70s, the United Farm Workers union and Cesar Chavez were petitioning to get increased wages from the growers. Pickers were making 50 cents an hour, and the time had come for them to get a raise, but not according to the growers or the Ku Klux Klan. Every month, farm workers were being found brutally murdered and thrown into streams. Proudly, the Dicks and our band, the Stains, did benefits at Raul's, and it was right up their alley, since the venue was Latino-owned.

Soon thereafter, in 1980, the Austin scene got all weird. At free public music gigs, Klan members started showing up and handing out brochures. The information was slanted to appeal to disaffected young people and explained how the Klan was a good bunch of people. Some other folks and I caught wind of this bullshit, confronted them, and told them to leave. It got very touchy, with a lot of shouting and shoving, but they got in their cars and drove away.

A planned Ku Klux Klan march was announced in the Austin

daily paper. The liberal powers encouraged people to stay away from the march. None of the church people and union people showed. So when the 50-strong Klan started to march, no one but the punks and a smattering of radicals resisted. They marched, and we showed up. I was pissed about this white-hooded blight upon my city marching down my street, so I threw a rock. More stones were thrown until 300 punks threw stones, so the Klansmen had to scurry along and finally cut short their little march as they ran back to their vehicles. Even the police seemed shocked at what the punks pulled off, but that didn't stop the cops from goose-stepping in and bloodying up some protestors. The dust soon settled, and like that, it was over, and they were gone. It was a very exciting and proud day to be an Austin punk rocker. I penned the song, "Born To Die" about the Klan in the next few days. They stopped coming to punk shows and stopped marching in Austin that day. *No War, No KKK, No Fascist USA.*

BORN TO DIE

I'm born to die
I'm born to fry
My life in a cage
Show my outrage
I'm misunderstood
I did what I could
I made my try
I was born to die

Goin' home
My mind is blown
I spilled my race
I found my case
I'm shot down on a fence
I'm dead in self defense
I live in a world of hate
With no regret a Nazi state
A racist dream, a world of hate
With no regret a Nazi state

No war
No KKK
No fascist USA

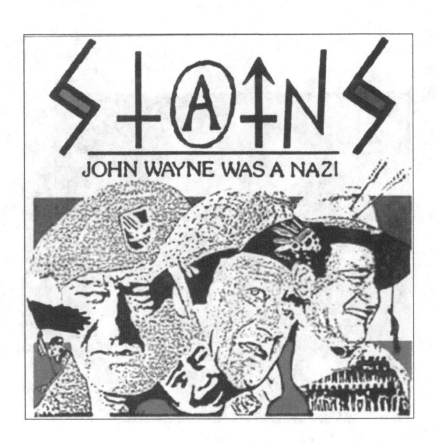

Oh, John Wayne, John Wayne

While living in Austin, my mom was still pushing me to finish school. I transferred the previous college credits earned in Tampa and Boston to the University of Texas, and started taking classes full-time. My major was American Studies, and I loved learning about how everything ticks and where I might fit into the mosaic of American culture. I was toying with the idea of eventually becoming a lawyer and fighting the system from within.

On June 11, 1979, the day of my college graduation ceremony, I found myself daydreaming in bed about it. I would not go, but I was curious. I didn't rent a gown. No one I knew was coming to see me. I didn't even know anyone else graduating either because I was hanging out with musicians who weren't all in school as full-time students, but I went over to the student union to sign up and pay to get my diploma in the mail so I could send it to my mom. That was done, so I just took in the sights of all the students in their gowns, milling around the student union.

I was hearing thousands of conversations all at once, and then a news announcement came across the large full-screen TV, "Last night John Wayne died of cancer," and the voice trailed off. The student union quieted up fast. My mind flashed on John Wayne, the movie character, his speeches, and his bravado. Then I thought of John Wayne, the "John Bircher," and his "white man's burden" view of Native Americans and

African Americans. And I flashed on that memory from childhood of him standing on the tank, criticizing the anti-war protesters. *Yuck*, I thought.

Then Franco appeared. He had a friend graduating. We were surrounded by hundreds of young, white Texans happy to be graduating. Then, all at once, a roomful of students started sobbing over John Wayne's death. Franco and I couldn't quite believe what we were witnessing. We lipped softly together at the same time, "John Wayne Was A Nazi," and started laughing and saying it over and over, louder and louder: "John Wayne was a Nazi. John Wayne was a Nazi!" We ran home to my house and wrote the song together. It rolled right off our lips, fingers, and tongues.

JOHN WAYNE WAS A NAZI

He liked to play SS
Kept a picture of Adolph
Tucked in his cowboy vest
Sure he would string up your mother
Sure he would torture your pa
Sure he would march you up to the wall
Sure he would hang you by your last ball

[chorus:]
He was a Nazi
But not anymore
He was a Nazi
Life evens the score

John Wayne slaughtered our Indian brothers
Burned their villages and raped their mothers
Now he has given them the white man's lord
Live by this or die by the sword

[chorus]

John Wayne killed a lot of gooks in the war
We don't give a fuck about John anymore
We all heard his tale of blood and gore
Just another pawn for the capitalist whore

[chorus]

John Wayne wore an army uniform
Didn't like us reds and fags that didn't conform
Great white hero had so much nerve
Lived much longer than he deserved

[chorus]

Late show Indian or Mexican dies
Klan propaganda legitimized
Hypocrite coward never fought a real fight
When I see John I'm ashamed to be white
Death bed Christian of this you avowed
If God's alive, you're roastin' now
Well, John, we got no regrets
As long as you died a long and painful death

Banned From Raul's

"Violent Redneck" is the shortest song on MDC's first album, and it is a manic burst of musical energy married to lyrics that tell the story of many ignorant asses who came into Raul's just looking for trouble and to start a fight. What these shit-heals didn't understand was how close knit the scene was. If six of them were to start a fight with one of us, then the entire club was going into battle to chase those fuckers right out into the parking lot and beyond. The punks ruled the roost at Raul's, and it was a good time... for a while.

By 1980, the Austin scene was split between the New Wavers and the Punk Rockers. Coming into the scene, I leaned a little New Wave due to my music tastes being more DEVO and Elvis Costello than Sham 69 and Vice Squad. Everybody loved the Sex Pistols, but that was almost the New Wavers' point: nobody was gonna top them, so why try? New Wave, as a music genre, was seen as broader, with more room for experimentation and growth. That line of reasoning sounded plausible, but punk just wasn't ready to go fuck off and die the death they all thought it should.

It didn't matter what my record collection looked like, I was making music that fell into the punk category. Plus the New Wavers looked down their noses at the punks, and, for that matter, kind of everyone else, too. Punk was dead, but some people just wouldn't admit so, and it was ruining their plans, darn it all!

Raul's was Austin's special club. Show dates had to be divided up between New Wave bands and punk ones. A guy named Steve Hayden took over Raul's around 1980. I don't know, maybe he bought it; if so, then, like a lot of club owners, especially in smaller cities, he saw the punks as somewhat of a pain in the ass and viewed the New Wavers as more advantageous because they were pretty hipsters who bought expensive drinks and caused few, if any, problems. New Wavers believed it was their time and felt offended: punk had the audacity to pretend it was still a happening thing.

Austin totally had that dynamic. Steve Hayden would dish most weekend nights out to the New Wave bands and, for the longest time, punk bands never got better than a Tuesday night. Of course, this made us punks feel isolated and disrespected, which in turn made us not respect the club, the rules, and the powers that be. Just at that time, hardcore was blowing up, with bands like Black Flag, DOA, Subhumans, and Fear playing Raul's. The punk hardcore thing was starting to get traction. Big Boys could roll either way and did well with both scenes. The Dicks, getting ever more popular, were also on a roll.

The desire to see punk gone was blinding some well-known Austin music critics, such as Ed Ward of the *Austin Chronicle* and Louis Black of the *Daily Texan*, who would put down the Dicks and the Stains by saying playing punk was like "flogging a dead horse." But the numbers and the enthusiasm weren't showing this. The horse had a pulse. The stick still had a purpose and a point to drive home. Punk seemed to be getting more popular by the month. Black Flag came to town, and some friends and I were slam dancing. Steve Hayden told me to stop or I'd be banned from the club. I friendly mock-pushed him, and he got his bouncer, Tuck; they escorted me to the door, and I was told that I was officially, "Banned from Raul's for life."

Banned for life from Raul's? Really? Really! A few times I went back, tried to apologize, but still I was not allowed in. A few months later, the club was running out of money. I'm not totally sure why, but then it was gone, and the scene moved to an old theatre downtown called Duke's Royal Coach. But just like that, it was 1981, Raul's was gone and it was tough for me to mourn. In the back of my mind, a thought was brewing: it was time to move to a new city.

Exene, John Doe, and Me

I was like dozens and dozens of guys through the years who have professed their love for Exene Cervenka of X. She is historical and appears early on in the film, *The Decline of Western Civilization*, as a hip and "desperate, get used to it," kind of woman. Also, Exene was cool, attractive, and one of the queens of American punk. So when X came to Austin in 1981, the Big Boys opened for them at Club Foot.

I am so there, I thought, as was most of the Austin scene. The Dicks were there. The Offenders were there. Everyone was there. We were all having a great time.

Big Boys did a cracking set: "Frat Cars," "Fun, Fun, Fun," and "Red/Green." Big Boys were such a great band, and they opened the doors of promoters for many bands, including MDC. Randy "Biscuit" Turner used to call me "David" with that thick Southern accent. They were great, and RIP Randy Turner, a gent and a beautiful man.

When X hit the stage, the crowd was ready. They start plowing through their set, ripping out "Johnny Hit and Run Paulene" and "The Once Over Twice." Everyone was into it. I was hanging with the Dicks, and we were all grooving completely. Then out of nowhere, there's this skinhead who looked a little like me. He ran up on the stage, grabbed Exene by her dress, and attempted to rip it off. John Doe threw off his guitar, grabbed the mystery skin, but he broke John's grip, dove into the crowd below, and a moment later he's nowhere to be seen. Then

Exene, scanning the crowd, spotted me, pointed, and screamed, "There he is!"

Before I knew it, everyone was looking my way as two bouncers started steaming their way through the crowd. I began to defend myself. Cindy Melbie and Buxf Parrot of the Dicks, who were with me the whole time, vouched for me, but due to Exene, John Doe, and Billy Zoom all screaming, "Get him out of here!" I was tossed out, literally, by my collar and belt. Moments later, I was in the alley, saying, "What the fuck?" But, oh well, that is that.

I decided to wait for my friends, and I knew the Big Boys were having a party, so I figured I'd go and hang. At the party, we were all there. Everyone, and I mean *everyone*, knew it wasn't me. Everyone said how weird it was and how no one recognized the guy, but they all knew it wasn't me. That made me feel better. I had a beer and thought, *Oh well, shit happens.*

A little later, we heard X was coming to the party and then they appeared. I chatted with the Big Boys, asked them to please let Exene know I was the person who was accused, and that I was friends with everyone, but it was not me.

"Please vouch that it wasn't me," I requested.

They conveyed the message, and I got into the vaguely defined queue everyone was in to meet X. When I arrived to where Exene and John were, once more she lets out a howl and shouts, "Get this fucking asshole out of my sight!" Well, it didn't take a bouncer to throw me out that time. I just peeled myself out of the scene, out of the room, and went home.

Some things are meant to be and others are not. That ended the big fat crush I had on Exene, and if there is a moral to this episode, it's that sometimes you're gonna get blamed for stuff you didn't do and hopefully you don't get jail time for it.

Getting the Hell Out of Austin

In 1981, small pockets of American Punk were coming together. Minor Threat became synonymous with DC; Black Flag, Fear, and Circle Jerks with LA; Reagan Youth with New York; DOA and the Subhumans with Vancouver, BC; Dead Kennedys and Flipper with SF; and then the smaller scenes: Dicks and Big Boys from Austin; Poison Idea of Portland; the Fartz from Seattle; Toxic Reasons and Zero Defects from Ohio; and Husker Du from Minneapolis.

DOA, the Subhumans, Black Flag, and Fear drove around the country, playing to a few hundred people in select hamlets. Before that, everyone's plan was to play local until a record company found you, and then you got backing, and hopefully they'd put you on some tour with someone like the Dead Boys, and you'd build your own following from there. Joe King Carrasco made it out of Austin this way. But with our brand, the new style of hardcore music, it flew over the rest of the music scenes' heads. Iggy Pop was much slower than hardcore.

As a band, we started contacting everybody we could get a hold of: we stayed in touch with Dave of Reagan Youth, whom I met at a Peppermint Lounge gig in NYC; I blindly wrote Minor Threat's Ian MacKaye just to let him know we existed and we dug his early project, Teen Idles. We met Black Flag and eventually put on a show for them in Austin. They wanted $400, and we worked so hard to make it happen with the Big Boys, the Dicks, the Offenders, and our band, the Stains.

BLACK FLAG

MILTOWN HIGH COW

SACCHARIN TRUST
Big Boys
STAINS
Dicks

BLACK FLAG from LA

REVENGE (lyrics: Greg Ginn)

Promises you made never became fact
We're gonna get revenge
You won't know what hit you
We're tired of being screwed
Don't tell me about tomorrow
Don't tell me what I'll get
I can't think of progress when
Just around the corner
There's a bed of cold pavement waiting for me
Revenge! I'll watch you bleed
Revenge! That's all I need
I won't cry if you die
Cause we're gonna get revenge
You won't know what hit you
We're tired of being screwed
Revenge!
Revenge!

ALSO FROM LA:

SACCHARIN TRUST

WITH THE Dicks AND STAINS MDC

THE Big Boys

AT: THE A.L.A. CLUB

SAT. NOV. 28

2 SHOWS!! 6 P.M. + 10 P.M.

RIVER

TOOMEY

A L A BALLROOM CLUB

BARTON SPRINGS Rd.

1 block NO. of BARTON Springs Rd - WEST off LAMAR on TOOMEY

It was a great show, and the first one I ever put on. I had so much help from the scene. It was such a victory.

This "Do It Yourself" or DIY scene happened because really no one else was going to do it. There was very few people in the beginning of the scene that were going to help out with your band's publicity, hang your flyers for the show, design your graphics, record your music and then send it out to media outlets, newspapers, magazines, provide you with a van and drive that van, and load that van. It was all to be done yourself.

This still goes on but way back it was a whole underground network that basically put on and advertised shows, traded records, the whole works. Zines came out of this philosophy. There was no internet, no cell phones — hell, computers and even answering machines weren't available outside of universities or multinational corporations. We had access to copiers and the post office and telephone landlines, and we made it happen.

Thousands of us have spent hours, days, years at Kinko's and the like making zines, flyers, word sheets, and even record sleeve creation. It was empowering and still is to realize if no one is gonna help, you just take the time and come up with the money to do it yourself. So if you're out there and want to get something creative going, I'd say, "Do it yourself."

We dreamed of touring, but who had heard of us outside of Austin? We put out 300 copies of the "John Wayne Was A Nazi" 7-inch single, with "Born To Die" on the B-side. It came to me to mail them to some zines that Inner Sanctum record shop had in their Austin store. *Flipside* in LA got one. I read in *Flipside* how Darby Crash died around New Year's. *Who's he?* I remember thinking.

I sent one to *Creep* magazine, and that was a good move. Mickey Creep lived with Jello Biafra from Dead Kennedys, and he got it, and Biafra played it for Tim Yohannan, who hosted a radio show called "Maximum Rock'n'Roll" that was syndicated to eight radio stations, so our little 'ol "John Wayne" single ended up making the radio charts on all of them. Tim Yohannan called and told me when our single hit number one.

This was exciting, but not as much as getting Jello Biafra's phone number to ask him if he would let the Dicks and Stains open for them. I called, and we got the gig: July 2, 1981 at San Francisco's Mabuhay Gardens. I then called Greg Ginn of Black Flag, and he gave us both opening slots at the Cuckoo's Nest in Costa Mesa for June, two weeks later. A tour of two shows! Boy, we were excited... I mean really, *really* excited. June was fast approaching.

We hit the road with our van, and my friend, Barbara Klatt, and her car, and my brand new Texaco credit card that I got for being a University of Texas graduate. Our adventure had begun.

Next thing I knew we were playing with our best buddies, the Dicks, at the Mabuhay Gardens for that hitherto unimaginably numerous punk crowd in San Francisco, and then Dead Kennedys played all their early stuff with Biafra crazily crab-crawling across the tables and rails. After the show, we hooked up with the Fuckettes – a group of gals connected with the band, the Fuck Ups — and set up a show with the Fuck Ups. We were staying with Timmy Yohannan, and met Jeff Bale and Ruth Schwartz, both major *Maximum Rocknroll* players. It was like instant friendships everywhere. San Francisco was a dream come true. We were the right band, in the right place, at the right time. Soup kitchens and punks could be found for miles and miles. We were on cloud nine.

After more than a month of this, we set off for our Cuckoo's Nest show south of LA. Of course, we had van problems, but still made it to the show just in time. The promoter wanted to kick us off the bill, but Greg Ginn wouldn't have it. It amounted to another over the top show with hundreds of kids. We met the LA Stains, who were overjoyed that we were changing our band name... but to what? We weren't sure. We had a great set, even played a couple of songs twice to beef up our 27-minute set.

As this was also Henry Rollins' first night as the lead singer of Black Flag, it quickly became an iconic night. He personified the psycho/ damaged lead singer. The band epitomized 1981 Black Flag: it tightly, intensely brought the audience to a hardcore rapture. What a moment. Then we jumped in the van and headed homeward back to Texas to settle on a band name, and decide how long before we moved to the Bay Area.

While kicking around band titles back in Austin, Buxf Parrot of the Dicks, said, "Millions of Dead Cops." It stuck, and there was no going back. The Stains became Millions of Dead Cops in July 1981, so the second printing of our 7-inch single came out under the name, MDC Stains. We had the band, we had the sound, and we had the name. We were ready.

After returning home to Austin, we needed to finish the album. We recorded in Houston with Dan Yaney. I don't think he ever recorded a hardcore band before, but you've gotta say he got it right. We had three different sessions with three different bass players. The Offenders weren't digging the time Mikey was spending with us, and they were his hometown brothers.

We went back into the studio with Franco Mares on one occasion, and with a fellow named Grant Gibson on another. The sessions went down very smooth, and for the first time I really got to hear what we sounded like. It sounded pretty amazing. In three sessions, we recorded and mixed the whole thing. It went down like clockwork, and I wish all my sessions in the studio were like that.

Carlos Lowry did the front cover art with the row of policemen, and Buxf Parrot did the illustration of the half Klansman/half policeman on the back cover. It was perfect.

We hooked up with an album presser, T.R., who would later fuck us over, kill R Radical Records, and rip off Flipside Records and Seven Seconds, but at least he introduced us to Geza X, who mastered our album and did a great job. We ordered the album covers in red, white, and blue, but the pressing plant did it in orange, white, and blue. We balked and they redid it correctly, so the red, white, and blue albums came out first to the world, but soon thereafter there was demand for more, so we used the orange, white, and blue covers a few weeks later. That worked out rather well for us.

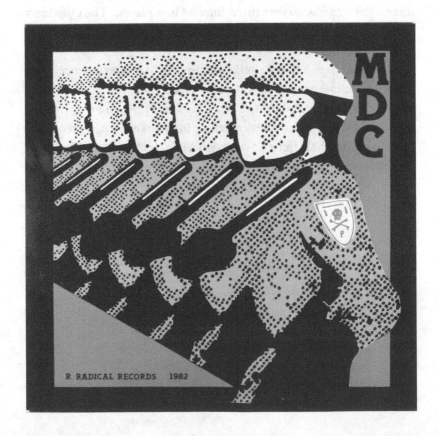

Leaving Austin was hard to do. Band members had girlfriends that weren't going with us, and Austin was simply hard to say goodbye to. Our friends in the Big Boys, the Dicks, the Butthole Surfers, DRI, Verbal Abuse, and others took it as a good sign that our Austin/Texas scene was busting out. Soon they would visit and some even stayed. Texas punk and hardcore had gained notoriety and respect. We were all packed up in late January 1982, singing "California, Here We Come." These were heady days, and it was damn exciting.

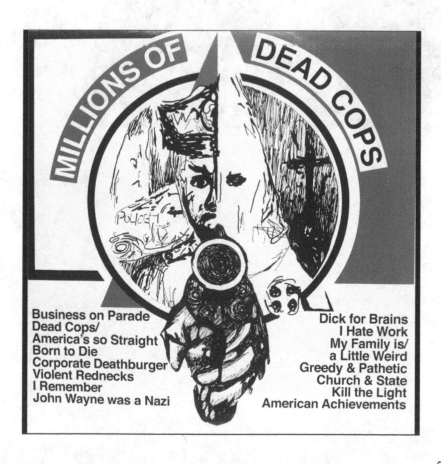

Soup Kitchens and San Francisco

San Francisco in 1981/1982 was truly a land to behold, a countercultural oasis attracting youth of all stripes to its bounty: teenage runaways, punk rockers, industrial art types like Mark Pauline of Survival Research Laboratories, college art types, and just young people everywhere we turned.

Everyone was trying to figure out how to survive but our new friends, the Fuckettes, had it wired. First, you get food stamps, and that amounted to $90 a month. I knew no one in Texas on food stamps; it was a cultural shift to get used to, being on the dole. Then you get on General Assistance, which was trickier, and they might require you to show up and clean city buses twice a week. People on General Assistance received $155 twice a month. Finally, you figured out where the soup kitchens were and when they were serving. Some kitchens, like the one at Hamilton Methodist Church in the Haight, served an early vegetarian lunch. There you could run into hundreds of punks, and it was glorious.

Everyone checked in with each other, like a tribal family of sorts. On Thanksgiving, you could eat with us: Gary Floyd and the Dicks, DRI, Verbal Abuse, the Fuckups, the Fuckettes, Condemned to Death, the SF Skins, Jaks Skate Team, Darren H. Peligro, and the poets, too, Diamond Dave, Tracey Anarchy, Kathleen Woods, Mitch the Bitch, Carol and the Lennon Brothers, Crucifix, the Witnesses, Dan Mackey, and Jenny Lush. Just hundreds and hundreds of punks. Kurt Brecht of Dirty Rotten Imbeciles was living in a tree. You could look him up in Golden Gate Park, literally.

A bunch of us punks moved into an abandoned beer brewery known as the Vats. It started out as a "work in exchange for rent" type of space. Many bands gravitated here very quickly, and with the power of word of mouth, all types followed. A lot of free places to crash were provided by that giant six-story building. It was the twilight of hobo punk heaven. It was here that I reconnected with Jenny Jo Brown, after meeting her years before as a college student in Tampa.

Many bands of various stripes were a part of this large warehouse space. There were punk shows, art exhibits, and studio spaces created. It started out very idealistic and tried to stay that way. Sadly, in time, with many of the bands being busy out on tour, many unsavory types – drug dealers, gang types, junkies, etc. – started moving in and abusing the space and its good residents. Someone suffered a drug overdose there, so the Vats showed up on the radar of city officials. Soon, everyone was evicted, and the building was gutted in 1984. Many people fondly remember the idealistic intentions of the residence, while others can't help but recall some of the unfortunate problems that occurred in such a free space.

One time in late 1982, Minor Threat came to town, and Ian held me to the cooked meal I had promised him when they fed us in DC. I took them to St. Martin de Porres soup kitchen to treat Ian to their famously rock hard grilled government cheese sandwiches, right before heading over to sound check and a hot show at the On Broadway. This was San Francisco's Golden Age, a time when the street punks shared everything, and we all looked out for each other. It was a special time. We didn't have much, but we had our scene. Many of the names mentioned are people that passed way too early. For those who are gone, RIP.

MAXIMUM ROCKNROLL

VOL. 1   NO. 1

MDC
MILLIONS OF DEAD COPS

MINOR THREAT

VICIOUS CIRCLE

JUVENIL JUSTICE

CHURCH POLICE

S/M NIGHTMARE

RIP RRZ?

AND

GOD FORBID.

POLITICS

NORTHERN CALIFORNIA COVERAGE

Bi- monthly

$1.00

62

Timmy Yohannan

Tim, who died in 1998, is dearly missed. Due to Tim's labors as a radio DJ, record releaser, fanzine editor, and as operator of Epicenter Records and 924 Gilman Street, he virtually created the DIY punk scene. He also served as ground zero for everything political punk. *Maximum Rocknroll* ran under him for a splinter shy of two decades, and it continues today for nearly two decades after he's been gone, selling hundreds of thousands of zines worldwide over the years.

Tim was enthusiastic, opinionated, a mover and a shaker, and a loyal friend. He would call you out on live radio and bad-mouth you to tens of thousands. He would lend you $5,000 the day after the ruble crashed to make sure your tour to Russia could happen. Tim Yohannan was my friend, he was MDC's friend, and he was a friend to regular punks whom he fought for by demanding lower door prices and an egalitarian attitude.

I wrote a song for him that appears on *Magnus Dominus Corpus*. Rest in Peace, dear sage.

TIMMY YO

This is a song for one of the godfathers of punk
All the rock star bullshit he wasn't afraid to debunk
Labeled himself a musical commie
When in fact he was everyone's mommy

Gave the kids a good place to go
And the unheard of bands somewhere to show
Now he is dead for over five years
Where's all the tributes for all your careers?

NOFX for years made their way
Laughing at what the political punks had to say
Taking the piss out of everyone's anger and passion
While being a shill for the Warped sneaker tour fashion

Epitaph, you make us cry and laugh
As you kick back and rake in the cash
You're the chief magnate of the music money machine
Yeah and you could say you fucked up the scene

Raking in fucking millions in dough
What does the scene have to show?
Shrewd businessmen, you made your big score
For the bands charging thirty dollars at the door

Well, you fat cats slap yourselves on the back
Your greed and pigishness are documented facts
You all think you're special and swell
Real punks everywhere hope you burn in hell

So this song is for you, Timmy, you were true blue
You could see where it was going, you already knew
Bad Religion hanging out with Britney Spears
Pink and Rancid helping each other's careers

Sell yourself out for better distribution
It's an old line, a shitty solution
Now you're part of the music conglomeration
Selling your punk attitudes to the whole nation

So I am sorry if it all doesn't mean shit to me
This music was supposed to set us free
Not to buy houses up in the Hollywood Hills
All you beautiful so talented people give me the chills

Bad Brains

How could anyone not like the Bad Brains and their singer, HR? Their music soared smooth, yet felt jagged. The songs jetted along so fast, athletic, and musically refined. HR could do backflips, and would do so in between verses. They were a sight to behold live. The "Pay To Cum" single is amazing. Plus, being an all African-American band, they carved out a unique place in American hardcore history. Wes Robinson, an East Bay promoter, asked us to open for them at Ruthie's Inn in Berkeley, California on April 1, 1982. We jumped to do it. That night we played and talked with the Bad Brains a little. Franco had a conversation with HR, and we were offered a spot to just drop everything and join them on tour. And we did.

That night we hopped in the van and drove pretty much straight through to Houston's Rock Island Club, roughly 2,000 miles away, in order to make it to the sound check 44 hours later. This is the same club where MDC had played with the Big Boys and Dicks in 1981.

We talked to the Bad Brains about having our friends, the Big Boys, set us up with a Tuesday gig in Austin on April 6th, with the Dicks on the bill, too. They gave the go ahead, and we called our friends to make it happen. We were tired by the drive and pretty much hung to ourselves at the show, except when HR decided to start talking to me about how females being on tour was all wrong and how women should be left at home, barefoot and pregnant. He also said that the way Tammy, our manager, was acting – meaning being on tour and carrying equipment

– would leave her with a barren womb as a curse from God. I almost couldn't believe my ears. It took me a little while to truly process. It seemed HR, my songwriting and musical hero, was spewing plain and simple vile sexism and misogyny.

The Houston show rocked with a full house and everyone felt good about how it went. After the show, both bands decided to meet up down the road in Austin. The Big Boy's Tim Kerr offered to put up the Bad Brains at his house. MDC got into town and we all had friends, loves, and folks we wanted to see, so we each went our own way and we didn't arrive at the gig until sound check, roughly two hours before the show.

From the minute I arrived, a weird vibe throbbed in the air. While we were unloading gear from the van, someone came out and told us that there was a problem going on inside with the Bad Brains. I went inside to see what was up, and was told HR had watched sound check and checked out the Dicks and the Big Boys, and he didn't like what he saw.

At this time, Gary Floyd and Randy Biscuit were two visibly out gay men and the punk scene in Austin loved 'em. And here was HR loudly complaining about sharing the same stage and microphone as these "blood clot faggot bands." Among Jamaicans, the phrase "blood clot" is a terrible insult.

HR's words got louder and weirder, and those of us in the Austin scene that were part of putting on the show just couldn't believe it. I tried to talk about it with HR, and he waved me away stating I brought him to a horrible place with horrible people.

It was ugly and it was surreal. After being vocal on the subject, HR disappeared back to his van, and the show went on. When it was time, he emerged and played his set. Somehow, we all made it through the night and the show went off well from the audience perspective. As I remember it, most people in the crowd of two hundred were unaware of what had gone down, and the rest of us went home scratching our heads, wondering what the hell that was about. Much like his misogynistic comments from the other night, it was again really crazy and tough to process, let alone understand.

The next day was the day of reckoning. MDC talked about what went down the night before. Each of us knew that this was wrong and that it was time to take a stand. We went to Tim Kerr's house and told the Bad Brains that we couldn't be part of a tour like this. We informed them, "We totally fucking disagree with you and if HR stands for 'Human Rights,' then how about human rights for everyone?"

HR tried to explain his heartfelt feelings on this matter: it was his religious belief and not something he felt could be compromised. I didn't have any scripture to back up my point-of-view, I just had my honest feelings about right and wrong. I believe that all people should be treated equally as human beings, regardless of gender or sexual orientation. Everyone gave from their hearts to set up, promote, and perform this show. It should have been an amazing experience for everyone, only to turn out far less than that. After what seemed like a few hours of round and round with no end in sight, we announced we were leaving the tour and eventually headed home to San Francisco.

Maximum Rocknroll and Tim Yohannan heard about what took place at our show in Austin, and asked if we would do an interview. We opened up about what took place, and the article generated a lot of attention and discussion when it was published.

I haven't had a real conversation with HR since the day after that show. We played a gig in Atlanta during the 1988 Democratic Convention, and HR was there, but he waved me away with a look of disdain. I recently heard he has expressed some regret on the topic. A lot of people have experienced sexist and/or homophobic thoughts at some point in their lives so personally evolving on this topic is all good. I applaud it and hold no grudges if that evolution is real.

MDC recently had an incident with a Southern California band where we dropped off a high paying gig with them over murderous, homophobic lyrics. Sexism, homophobia, and racism might have noticeably improved in the four decades of punk rock that I have been involved, but still exist today. Taking a stand on these issues are some of my proudest moments in my band's history.

MDC Tour with Bad Brains

April 1 – Berkeley, CA: Ruthie's Inn: Bad Brains + Code of Honor + MDC

April 3 – Houston, TX: Island: Bad Brains + Really Red + MDC

April 6 – Austin, TX: Esther's Pool: Bad Brains + Big Boys + Dicks + MDC

Spring, Summer, Fall

After the Bad Brains nightmare, we made the long drive back to the Bay Area. There never has been an upside for what went down between the Bad Brains and us. Some people even suggested we set them up on purpose, which we never did. It is what it is, and we warned others. We traveled over 4,000 miles to make a couple hundred dollars. We just wanted to get home and work on what was to become the *Multi Death Corporation* EP. So home we went, and did some great shows with Hüsker Dü, the Big Boys, Black Flag, and DOA. We also did a show at The Barn in Alpine Village outside LA on July 3, 1982 with Dead Kennedys, Minor Threat, the Zero Boys, and the Detonators. A *Flipside* poll voted it "Los Angeles Gig of the Year": it was a great show, maybe our best bill ever.

We were so casual about what we were doing. We were in the middle of creating something that we knew was profound. From that Alpine Village gig, we started a cross-country tour. We played the Whisky-A-Go-Go with DOA; that's the gig where Fat Mike said he heard "John Wayne Was A Nazi," but "all the other songs kinda suck," and wrote about it in a NOFX song. I truly beg to differ. I stand by our 100 or so songs. I did pay him back by calling him a shill for the sneaker fashion tour in "Timmy Yo."

We did chat with each other at the back of shows around 1989, and he clearly saw things were going "melodicore." I could see the new reality that hardcore was disappearing, especially political hardcore in the early '90s. But I do what I do, and I am what I am. To his true credit, Mike put out one of my side projects, the Submissives record, *An Anvil Will Wear Out Many A Hammer*, as well as a kinda-lost MDC 7-inch project named "Pig Champion," in the mid-'90s on his label, Honest Don's, a division of Fat Wreck Chords.

On August 4, 1982, we played El Paso for about 200 Marines heading over to Lebanon a few days later. At first, the crowd seemed standoffish towards us, but I said, "Hey, we're punks, and you're Marines, and society thinks we're both out of our minds."

I paused and added, "My heart is with you guys," and then we had a dance contest. MDC morphed into the Marine Death Corps. They friggin' loved it. They danced on the floor like the toga partiers from *Animal House*, and we all had a great time. I realized that we were more than a hardcore band; we were really a people band that wanted to touch everyone. We felt we were like the Blues Brothers "on a mission from God."

The next night we played Austin with Dead Kennedys, Big Boys, the Dicks, and the Offenders. Austin's scene was flying high, and we were still a part of it. Gary played in cowgirl drag using the name "Pammy Floyd." It was a fabulous performance. We gigged the next two nights with Dead Kennedys, which was like playing in a punk rock circus, to between three and five thousand people. It was such an honor to open for them. All of a sudden for us, their crowd was our crowd, and it was just plain old intoxicating.

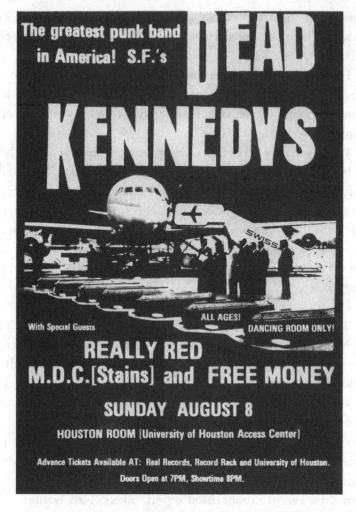

The greatest punk band in America! S.F.'s
DEAD KENNEDYS

With Special Guests

ALL AGES!
DANCING ROOM ONLY!

REALLY RED
M.D.C.[Stains] and FREE MONEY

SUNDAY AUGUST 8

HOUSTON ROOM [University of Houston Access Center]

Advance Tickets Available AT: Real Records, Record Rack and University of Houston.
Doors Open at 7PM, Showtime 8PM.

We went up to Chicago and then played Minneapolis with Hüsker Dü at First Avenue and 7th Street Entry. The place was packed. I felt like Prince was gonna show up, mount the stage, and do a few bars of "Purple Rain." Minneapolis raged that night.

Next, we headed over to a gig in East Lansing, Michigan, where Doc Crucifuck baited the local police with our band's name. He made a flyer that listed recent Police Academy graduates, drew x's over their eyes, and wrote "future dead cops" on top of the flyer. Boy, did the cops seek us out. Luckily, our friend Vicky's mother told them she was chaperoning our stay. A cop looked at me with his flat, dead pig eyes and said, "Don't be surprised when you get buried in one of these corn fields." Fuck... SCARY!

From there we headed east and played the Gallery East in Boston with SS Decontrol, and we were introduced to their Boston fans' moshpit pyramid pig pile, which was truly awesome. We also met Al Quint of Suburban Voice fame.

We played a few other East Coast gigs before heading back to NYC to play with Reagan Youth and a version of the Beastie Boys called the Imperial Knights of Schism. They were taking the piss out of the Rastafarians, and the Bad Brains threw eggs intended for us at them. I started chatting with a few of the Bad Brains' friends, and I said I wasn't looking to fight because I wished for it all to just be over. This kind of worked for all of them, but HR still looked at me hard, and I just shrugged.

The next day we headed north to play a Trans-Canadian Tour starting in Montreal and heading to Ottawa, Toronto, London, Windsor, Winnipeg, and Calgary. We loved down-home Canadians. Still do. We played these old hotels that were cheap watering holes for drinking, and then cheap places to sleep when you decided you were too drunk to drive.

One of these joints was the Calgarian Inn. Here you got to play a week, three times a day, and sleep in a couple of the broken down rooms. That's a special kind of insane to play a total of 21 live sets over seven days. We had drunken oil riggers, bikers, First Nations folks, working women, and about 30-odd young people come to check out the band. All this and get paid $2,000 for the week. You could play a slew of loser gigs and make up for it with a week in Calgary.

About this time we started dialing Biafra three times a week to see if we could get on Dead Kennedys' European tour. We called and called and called, but Biafra had said both Flipper and DOA had been asked, and we had to wait to see what their answers would be. Week-in, week-out we checked in with him and, finally, we got on the tour. What an incredible year 1982 was turning out to be. Next, we had to figure out how we were going to pay for tickets, figure out transportation, and all the rest as well.

First European Tour, 1982

MDC getting on this tour was the icing on the cake of an unbelievable year, just amazing. Like many in the music business who get just so hot, we got to experience being Cinderella, but we still had to buy airplane tickets, try to release our album in Europe, and figure out transportation. We also had to figure out how to live and get around on 100 quid a day, approximately $200, which was our pay. We had to get to know the members of Dead Kennedys and figure out how much we could depend on them.

We were street punks that lived in the Vats and ate at soup kitchens. Situations would crop up where we just didn't understand the way business was done. We were having the tour of our lives but noticed opening bands didn't get the same volume out of the PA as headliners. MDC came from an egalitarian background in which even-splits with the Dicks or Big Boys was taken for granted. When we hooked up with the sound guy, Chris, he hinted around at first, but finally explained we were getting only forty percent of the PA. Hence, we sounded weak compared to the headliners. Apparently, that's a normal routine in professional music. Queen's opening bands suffered it, too, and so did everyone else. We were clueless, couldn't believe it, and were just plain old hurt.

We had handed the MDC album off to Alternative Tentacles UK to release in time for the tour. That never happened. We hadn't experienced labels planning an album to come out eight months to a year in the future. We were disappointed to do the tour without our music to sell.

Music industry professionals are focused on making the headliners shine because that's their bread and butter. Since then I have figured out that is the way the professional music world works. We were no longer in our hometown where everyone looks out for each other. As well, Biafra worked with a man named Bill Gilliam, who booked this tour and ran Alternative Tentacles UK. He exuded the "I work for the big guys, and you blokes, not so much" attitude.

Looking back, I realize we were like grumbling country bumpkins who started counting the slights, like being locked out of backstages and having no backstage food, yet the tour still felt extraordinary. I am incredibly grateful Biafra made that tour possible. Like I said, I wish our lack of grace could just disappear, but I must own it.

Liverpool, Sheffield, Leeds, Leicester... Northern England was magnificent! All of England was fabulous. We drove a small Opel rental car, thousands of people flocked every show, people took us home from gigs, we met fans and had phenomenal fun. English punk culture was totally over the top and going crazy. Fans adored Dead Kennedys, and a lot of love rolled down to us though in Leicester, national movement skinhead thugs attacked the crowd, MDC, and Dead Kennedys.

I hadn't really noticed any problems at the show. I was backstage in a happy bubble, meeting people, and warming up my voice. When it was our turn, I hit the stage and I could feel a weird energy in front of the stage as some very big skinheads started giving me the finger with some very hard looks. I was pacing the stage, belting out my lyrics, and getting into my performance. I hadn't noticed till it was too late that a few of these guys were up on stage where they grabbed me and carried me out into the crowd. There, on the ground in front of the stage, I was getting hit and kicked by six to eight big skinheads. At a certain point, I was knocked unconscious and taken to the hospital.

I came to with an attractive British nurse smiling down at me and cautioning me to relax. I loved that moment waking to that nurse and her soft voice. I thought for a second that I had died and went to British nurse heaven. Rumors circulated that the Exploited were somehow involved with stirring up the National Movement thugs at this show. Whether this is true or not, I have no idea.

One night, after our gig in Bath, we stayed with Disorder in their squat. I lost my crew of people when we got there; I had been messing around in the rental car, getting my stuff together. When I looked up, everyone had disappeared. I started calling out, hoping someone would hear me. Soon enough, I was found by Chaos of the band, Chaos UK, and that's something we've laughed about many times since.

The Bath/Bristol area has many great punk bands, past and present. The Subhumans and Amebix are another two legendary bands from that area. It's a lovely place (and an hour and a half from Stonehenge, to boot). On November 23rd, we played Brighton, the hometown of Peter and the Test Tubes Babies. We slept at Peter's house, and they were very nice people. We had a wonderful time. Then we played Northeastern England and Norwich. We met and played with the Subhumans at the Polytechnic in London. We met Phil Free and Steve Ignorant of Crass, and we chatted each other up hard and were invited to their farm north of London.

London is such a large place, but people are friendly. They like Americans and feel we are their cousins of sorts. They hang out in pubs and on the street. Taking it all in, my head swam. We did an interview with poet and journalist Attila the Stockbroker that was released in *Sounds*, a weekly music rag, which gave us a big spread with photos.

We had one more gig in England in South Hampton. This was more of a wealthy area and the gig lacked that certain "je ne sais quoi" of other British gigs. All and all, I was having the best time of my life. Not to knock England, but it did have one weird thing going on. The punks there, in general, loved to spit their phlegm at you almost like they were in a horseshoe contest and your head was the stake. We did not miss that… or maybe the better metaphor would be darts. The British do love their darts. Bull's eye! Loogie in Dave's eye! From there, we crossed the North Sea into Belgium, where, on my 24th birthday, we played a Brussels suburb for 1,500 Belgian groovers. It was mainland cool.

The next night we shook up the Amsterdam's famous stone Paradiso Rock Hall, and the Dutch folks dug it so much. We received a lot of transferred love from the Kennedys. Amsterdam is another really special place: historically, in the 1500s and 1600s, a Protestant stronghold of ideas in an ass-backwards world. If you go, while there go eat at the Milkweg, where Dan from Die Kreuzen runs the restaurant. For fun, lightheartedly flirt with everyone who has a nose piercing... this will keep you busy. Oh yeah, go see a Rembrandt and a Van Gogh, if not something more modern.

Next, we hit Hamburg, Germany, on December 6th, playing a giant place with 4,000+ people creating one hot crazy night. Hamburg is very cool, known for its famous Reeperbahn red light district and the infamous Hafenstrasse Squat, which has hosted us many times through the subsequent years. We arrived at Friedrich-Elbert Hall very early and waited at the front door. People started to just assume we were the Dead Kennedys. People professed their love assuming I was Biafra. Before too long, the Dead Kennedys' security ushered us inside.

More than once on this tour with the Dead Kennedys, standing outside the hall, our typical conversations would go like this:

DK fans would ask, "Hello, you are the Dead Kennedys?"

To which we'd reply, "No, we're not, we're MDC, but we'll be opening for them tonight."

Then they'd reply, "Then you are Jello Biafra?"

I'd answer, "No, but he'll be here playing tonight."

Then they'd turn to their friends, converse in rapid-fire German. Soon dozens of misinformed, non-English-speaking Europeans with pen and paper would mob us, saying, "You are so super," and ask, "Please make autograph."

We would try to straighten this out to no avail. I'd wind up signing, "To Fritz, Best Wishes from a close personal friend of Jello Biafra."

I tried to fight it for a while, but at a certain point I snapped and when asked, I'd say, "Of course I'm," and then quietly mumble, "a close personal friend of," and then loudly again, "Jello Biafra." I hugged and kissed hundreds of them. I might be going out on a limb, but I think

Americans everywhere would have been proud to see how I represented American punk rock. So what if there was a minor misunderstanding concerning just exactly who was who?

My band, on the other hand, started distancing themselves from me, viewing my behavior as some sort of deviant neurosis. I didn't care. Truly, I reveled in it.

At the Rotation Club in Hannover, the night after Hamburg, you could fall into a moat way below the stage, not one filled with water but extending like a black abyss going nowhere. As we nailed our set, I watched guys trying to creep up from the crowd to where we were on the stage. Sure enough, one by one, they would misstep and slide down into the darkness. Whoever designed this place was not considering punk rock. A lot of folks, well, they just didn't make it, and dropped out of sight into the moat. I didn't see them again. The gig was really weird for me, contemplating where they ended up while belting out our set.

Next we traveled by train to West Berlin, traveling from West Germany through communist East Germany until we arrived in West Berlin. Berlin, at the time, had a lot of Hitchcock, scary, noir flavor to it. With its totalitarian government, the East German police/army could alternate from looking like they wanted to kill you to looking like they wanted to throw off their uniforms and join you at gigs. One young German army lad was trying to interpret our name, and in a flash he got it and smiled very hard at us. He said he liked the name Millions of Dead Cops "very, very much."

Berlin once was a center of the world, and has become one again. It was trippy to hang out late in the Kreuzberg section as East German tower guards stared down at us. Growing up there at that time must have been hectic. It was so on the edge. Punks partied like it was the end of the world. Anyway, when I stepped outside the show, I saw kids on their way to getting beer were casually throwing rocks at armored police trucks. The police didn't respond. I was taken aback and couldn't believe that the cops didn't react. It was a way more passive, non-confrontational way of dealing with rocks being thrown at them than in the US, where heads would've gotten busted. Berlin through the years has been put through the ringer. I love Berlin.

As the tour continued, our relationship with the Kennedys started to sour, due to us, mostly. At the time, we very much acted like know-it-alls. We were vegan/vegetarians and could be hypercritical, opinionated, and were certainly limited and narrow in our experiences of the ins and outs of a larger rock world than we had been involved with previously. We learned a lot.

MDC, on our own, pulled off a little show in Munich and visited Dachau. Concentration camps are heavy bummers but a must for political bands, really all bands and all people. Some ghostly, haunting shit can be seen there.

A Dutch record store owner, Hank Schmidt, hooked us up a final show in Arnhem, Holland, on December 15th with Jesus and The Gospelfuckers, a Dutch street punk band along the lines of San Francisco's The Fuck Ups. These guys were wild. They were intoxicated nearly all the time, giving the finger and mouthing off to Dutch police. Some Dutch police can be very tolerant, something I was not used to, coming from the States.

When we traveled from Berlin to Nuremburg for our last meeting with Dead Kennedys, we hooked up with some local women from Berlin, Jenny and Arrabella, who had a van. Instead of going by train from West Berlin through East Germany and back into West Germany, we drove on the East German autobahn. That ride on the autobahn was eerie. Back then, before the Berlin Wall came down, when driving through East Germany, you were supposed to stay in a certain lane. The highway was very monitored, Cold War style, and there was nowhere to stop except for little gas station restaurants.

At one of these stops, I went into the restaurant with Jenny and Arrabella to order some french fries to go. By accident, I don't know how, I stood too close to a Christmas tree decorated in homemade ornaments. Unawares, I must've brushed against it and tinsel hanging on the tree grabbed onto my jacket. When I moved, the tree clung, pulled off balance, toppled and fell over flat, *Crash!*

Fuck, I was freaked and quickly walked my ass back to the van in the parking lot, but before long there were stern East German police ready to crack the head of an American punk Xmas-tree destroyer. My bandmates started humming the TV show theme song to *Hogan's Heroes*. At the time, it was funny, even though I didn't know what they would do to me.

Luckily, Jenny interceded in German, and – roughly translated — said, "The clumsy American is sorry. What should he do?" A fine was arranged, a small payment accepted, and they wrote me some kind of a bull-in-a-China-shop ticket. All I wanted was some fries.

Our drive ended at the docks, to take the night ferry back to England across the wintry North Sea. Nobody warns you about the rough seas, and everyone loaded up on food before they got on board. Well, we did too, along with our shipmates. When we were out just a few miles offshore into the North Sea, the boat started swaying, surging, pitching, yawing, and heaving, so nearly everybody aboard puked up their din-dins. The boat was wall-to-wall puke. It smelled like puke, it looked like puke, and I was praying helicopters would rescue us off the awful puke boat. Here's another lesson for everybody: the helicopters are never there to rescue you, just like during Hurricane Katrina in New Orleans. My advice is "Don't stuff yourself before departing on a winter ferryboat ride, especially in the North Sea."

After our rough ride on the puke ferry, Crass invited us to their farm, which became a warm homecoming with the band we most admired. Penny was wonderful. Gee Voucher was warm and shared her art easily, and the night just rolled on. They served a delicious vegan Shepherd's Pie. I enjoyed the company of Steve Ignorant and Phil Free very much. It was a pleasant time. Penny expressed his desire to change Millions of Dead Cops to My Dear Constable. That really does have a pacifist cool ring to it. As much as Penny liked us individually, the Dead Cops had too violent an edge for him. Yet, he got us.

Al came up with "Multi Death Corporation," so we devised the new EP project. I attempted to flirt with Eve Libertine, who shut that right down pronto, and told me she didn't like the skull imagery in our art either. At least she didn't yell at me and call me an asshole like another punk rock crush. It was a beautiful night that I'm glad we got to have, but in no time it was over, and we were off by train back to London.

We played eighteen European shows with Dead Kennedys, met and ate with Crass at their farm, and flew home to New York for Christmas to figure out our next move. Life was pretty good for MDC in 1982.

European Tour: MDC, Dead Kennedys + Peter and the Test Tube Babies
Nov 15 – London: Musician's Collective: MDC (No Nukes Benefit)
Nov 17 – Liverpool: The Warehouse: Dead Kennedys + Peter and the Test Tube Babies + MDC + Mayhem
Nov 18 – Sheffield: The Leadmill: Dead Kennedys + Mau Maus + MDC
Nov 19 – Leeds: Leeds Polytechnic: Dead Kennedys + MDC + Xpozez
Nov 20 – Leicester: Percy Gee Building: Dead Kennedys + MDC + 13th Chime
Nov 22 – Bath: Bath Pavilion: Dead Kennedys + MDC + Disorder
Nov 23 – Brighton: Moulscombe Polytechnic: Dead Kennedys + PTTB + MDC
Nov 24 – Norwich: University of East Anglia: Dead Kennedys + PTTB + MDC + Serious Drinking
Nov 26 – London: Central London Polytechnic: Dead Kennedys + MDC + Serious Drinking + Subhumans
Nov 27 – London: Central London Polytechnic: Dead Kennedys + MDC + Serious Drinking
Dec 1 – South Hampton: West Refectory: Dead Kennedys + PTTB + MDC
Dec 4 – Mechelen, Belgium: Voksbelang: Dead Kennedys + MDC
Dec 5 – Amsterdam, Holland: Paradiso: Dead Kennedys + MDC
Dec 6 – Hamburg, Germany: Friedrich-Elbert Hall: Dead Kennedys + MDC + Napalm
Dec 8 – Recklinghausen: Musikpalast: Dead Kennedys + MDC
Dec 9 – Hannover: Rotation: Dead Kennedys + MDC
Dec 10 – Berlin, Germany: SO 36: Dead Kennedys + MDC + Sick Pleasure

ROCK AGAINST REAGAN

a free music & comedy concert

with **Dead Kennedys**

MDC

Permanent Wave

Sticks Against Stones

Emcees: Jane Dornacker, Tom Ammiano, Lea DeLaria with Jeanine Strobel

And Comics: Ruby "Rodriguez" Rubenstein, Whoopi Goldberg, and Will Durst.

SUNDAY, OCTOBER 23, 1983, 1-7 pm

Dolores Park, 18th & Dolores

Rock Against Reagan Tour, 1983

The Yippies, also known as the Youth International Party, were leftover radicals from the 1960s and 1970s. Based in NYC, founded originally by a collective that included Abbie Hoffman, Jerry Rubin and Paul Krassner, and best known for disrupting the 1968 Democratic Convention in Chicago, were joined in the '80s by a new young breed of activists, and some of them were hip to hardcore. MDC met Alan Thompson and Christy Robb, total activists who lived their entire lives trying to affect change.

The Yippies offered us a tour with a political subtext: they wanted to legalize or, at least, decriminalize marijuana and get apathetic marginalized youth (that is, punk rockers) registered as voters to help oust Reagan from the Oval Office in the 1984 election. They let us help build the tour, and sometimes the shows themselves, with other bands. We could do our own shows between Yippie shows to raise extra tour money, and local Yippies were supposed to raise money to put on the shows, and hopefully get the touring bands gas and food stipends. We recommended the Dicks, DRI, and the Crucifucks. They already were hooking up Dead Kennedys and Reagan Youth for the bigger shows. Each community reflected the Yippie leadership of the different scenes. We hit the road with the four players in MDC plus two of our best buddies: manager Tammy Lundy and resident artist Lisa Smith of Toronto. It doesn't sound like much now, but in this era, just about no touring hardcore bands traveled with women. We didn't think of it as groundbreaking; we just realized it was much cooler to have them around. Boy band world can be very boring. It lacks balance. We were always a *Powerpuff Girls* band and still are.

Our first gig in Madison, Wisconsin, was organized by a first-rate gent who recently died of lung cancer. His name was Ben Masel, and he had us play on the state capital steps in front of 5,000 people. We co-headlined with Bucky the Marijuana Badger. Thousands of joints were thrown out into the crowd, and we experienced a grand old hippie activist time. Ben was the master of setting up protests and actions, and whenever the police overreacted, he would be there filming it and then have a lawsuit that he would win. Those would fund operations until their next captured-on-tape lawsuit was planned. Cops never seem to learn, do they? Next was Springfield, Illinois, then Carbondale, both much smaller events, but the people there were appreciative, and the tour rolled on.

The next day we played Chicago with Minor Threat and Articles of Faith in a non-Rock Against Reagan event. Vic Bondi interviewed Ian MacKaye and myself in a classic interview that ran in *Maximum Rocknroll*. Ian is one of the nicest, straight-up folks I have ever met, a real alert dude. Vic Bondi is a special guy as well, down-to-earth, and a straight shooter. No bullshit. If you want to read it, do an internet search for the Ian MacKaye, Vic Bondi, and Dave Dictor interview, and it should come up.

The show itself was epic. Chicago is always a rollickin' town. Next up, we gigged in Columbus, Ohio, on the state capital steps – a big gig – but with less overall character compared to the Madison Bucky the Badger show. Still, thousands of people hung out everywhere. Ohio, our kind of people, supported six shows scattered throughout different parts of the state.

We played with the Dicks in Akron at one of the best little scenes going in 1983; Jimi Imij's band, Zero Defects, and Vince Packard's PPG were also on the bill. Vince is the great artist who drew the Multi Death Skull Tank art for our first EP. This was an intensely fervent scene. The crowd hoisted Gary Floyd up on their shoulders and carried him around the room as the Dicks did a version of the Crosby, Stills, Nash, and Young song "Ohio" with the line about tin soldiers and Nixon.

Detroit and Cleveland amounted to small shows. Detroit was always a rough town for us. Whenever we were around, it crawled with skinheads, fights erupted in the audience, and once our van was vandalized. In Cleveland, a band called Starvation Army simply hated MDC. I was never exactly sure why, maybe because we were political and they were not. Thus they slagged us as often as they could. What can you say to that but "Oh, well?"

In New York City, we played on a flatbed truck that started at Washington Square Park. The Yippies tossed handfuls of joints into the crowd as we played while being slowly driven up Fifth Avenue. The sights and sounds were incredible, and the people in those neighborhoods got an eyeful and earful. Doc Crucifuck performed the song "Democracy Spawns Bad Taste" to school kids, tourists, and United Nations types. I assume you can't get a permit to do that kind of unique, bombastic gig anymore.

The following day we played a field in Central Park with the Dicks and Crucifix, always a cool band. May 13th we played the Love Club in Philadelphia, an action packed gig. I suffered a nasty chip taken out of my front tooth so I learned a big lesson about holding a microphone and protecting my mouth.

The May 15th show at Boston Common was incendiary. DRI just ripped it the fuck up, and the Boston kids, seeing them for the first time, went nutso.

The daytime gig in Amherst, Massachusetts, was a big outdoor gathering. The police tried to cut the show short. I directed the crowd to surround the generator so they couldn't turn it off, and we finished our set. This felt like a solid victory celebrating Rock Against Reagan – people power in action protecting the power supply!

On May 25th, we played with the great Papa Jerry Williams. He recorded a lot of the early Bad Brains stuff and would, a few days later, record our four-song *Multi Death Corporation* EP. Papa Jerry's in the film *American Hardcore*, and people that knew him absolutely adored the man. A real true soul, RIP, friend.

The Beacon Theatre is a 2,500-seat hall in midtown Manhattan, a real classic theatre where we played on June 4th with Dead Kennedys and False Prophets: a stupendous show.

On June 14th in NYC, we played a street party in the Alphabet City in lower Manhattan. People had it hard there, but it was a cool scene. The Latino kids totally loved us. It was really down-home NYC street life circa 1982, back when you could walk into an empty store, put $10 into a hole in the wall, and lo and behold! the money was gone and a dime's worth of pot appeared.

On June 24th, we played in Virginia with White Cross at the

University of Richmond. It was a special time, and I envisioned Richmond as one of those small southern cities like Austin, Raleigh, and Jacksonville. Two stars in Richmond, David Brockie of Gwar (Rest in Peace, sir) and a drag queen named "the Dirt Woman," were on site. She was part Divine and part all-Southern girl. She lit up the room and was quite a character. I hear she is still in Richmond strutting her stuff.

July 3rd featured 10,000 people at the Lincoln Memorial in Washington, DC. Cops roamed all over the place, hassling people every which way; meanwhile, across the lawn a couple hundred yards away, Ronald Reagan's Independence Day holiday bash with Wayne Newton was happening. The difference in appearance between the two crowds was amazing. We were punk/denim types, and they were bright colors and checkered shirts.

At our show, great bands played one after the other. Dead Kennedys stole the show with their set of early songs from *Fresh Fruit for Rotting Vegetables*. Hearing "Chemical Warfare," "Kill the Poor," and "Police Truck" at the Lincoln Memorial was way cool. MDC, DRI, Toxic Reasons, Reagan Youth, the Crucifucks, Cause for Alarm, and even more bands all rounded out the bill.

I will never forget Biafra pointing at the helicopter buzzing around the Washington Monument late during his set and remarking, "The Washington Monument is the shape of a Klansman's hood to remind us that George Washington owned slaves." Pretty profound there, Mr. Biafra.

Apr 24 – Madison, Wisconsin / Capital Steps: MDC, Crucifucks
Apr 25 – Springfield, Illinois / Capital Grounds: MDC, Crucifucks
Apr 27 – Carbondale, Illinois / University of Illinois: MDC, Crucifucks
Apr 29 – Chicago / Centro Americano: Minor Threat, MDC, Articles
   of Faith (not a RAR gig)
Apr 30 – Columbus, Ohio / Capital Grounds: MDC, Dicks, Crucifucks
May 1 – Detroit / City Club: MDC, Dicks, Crucifucks
May 6 – Cleveland/City Hall: MDC, Dicks, Crucifucks
May 7 – New York City / Flatbed Truck to UN Plaza: MDC, Crucifucks
May 8 – NYC / Central Park: MDC, Dicks, Crucifix, Crucifucks
May 13 – Philadelphia / Love Club: MDC, Dicks, Crucifucks (not a
   RAR gig)
May 15 –Boston Common: MDC, DRI, Dicks, Crucifucks
June 4 – NYC / Beacon Theatre: Dead Kennedys, MDC, False
Prophets
   (not a RAR gig)
June 9 – Providence / Living Room: MDC, DRI (not a RAR gig)
June 14 – NYC/street party: MDC, DRI, Reagan Youth, Cause For
   Alarm, Agnostic Front (not a RAR gig)
June 17 – *Multi Death Corporation* EP recorded with Papa Jerry
June 18 – Pogoes: MDC, DRI, Cause for Alarm (not a RAR gig)
June 24 – Richmond, VA: MDC, DRI, White Cross
July 2 – NYC /Block Party (not a RAR gig)
July 3 – Washington DC / Lincoln Memorial: Dead Kennedys, MDC,
   DRI, Crucifucks, ODFX, et al

After July 3rd

Wow, we had been touring our tails off straight from early spring1982 yet still got in the van and kept rolling down the road and playing. We headed north to play with the DK's and DRI at the Reggae Club on July 5th in lower Manhattan. In this period, we were still getting a lot of opening slots with Dead Kennedys.

In Europe, Alternative Tentacles UK had finally released our first album, after Dead Kenedys' members, Klaus and Ray, had re-mastered it. We decided as a band to keep our tour difficulties with the DKs to ourselves. We avoided all negative comments in interviews about the tour.

Mid-July led us into a disastrous tour into Canada, where two of us were busted, and the police messed with us, ruining our tour. We played Quebec City twice, and in Montreal with GBH. We hung out with Colin and the boys, who were very friendly and still are, when we see them at Rebellion Festivals and such. We played Ottawa with Porcelain Forehead, and then went to Toronto for two shows.

In Toronto, Franco and Ron double-parked in front of a post office. They were stopped, searched, and charged with "Weapons Dangerous to the Public's Safety." Having searched our van, the police construed that the jack and tire irons were dangerous weapons, even though they sat in the wheel wells included with most motor vehicles. That messed us up financially. Thanks again to Ruth Schwartz for helping us. A lot.

In Toronto, the police found the box with our Millions of Dead Cops buttons, and they hated those things. For the third time in my life, while at the police station arranging for bail, a policeman told me these buttons were gonna get me buried in a field somewhere. Third time is not always the charm. I love Canada, but the Canadian police just hated punk rock. When we finally got everyone out, we headed to DC to play with Iron Cross. I was in a daze and remember very little.

Finally, we figured it was time to go home to patch our bones. Somewhere along the line, Target Video asked to film us and Crucifix on September 3rd. Crucifix were a bunch of super nice guys doing that D-beat British sound, with Sothira Pheng the lead singer, Jimmy Crucifix on guitar, Matt Burroso on bass, and Chris Douglas on drums. They were very political, too, which we admired. For a band that only played four years, they made their mark.

One time, we were traveling on the LA freeway and saw the LA Highway Patrol surrounding Crucifix's van. We soon noticed the cops posing with the tall mohawked members of Crucifix for pictures. LA cops do suck, but that was pretty amusing.

This video was distributed around the world, and we love the association with Sothira and the guys, but we have never gotten a cent from Target, and I don't think anyone has. Anyway, that's me in the white, Klan-cop t-shirt. Also, *Flipside* videotaped us with the Dicks and Subhumans at the Olympic Auditorium in front of 5,000 fans. The gigs at the Olympic were like rugby matches, with fans taking over the stage and crashing at full force into me and the band. The stage security just gave up. I was pretty beat-up at this show.

We experienced interpersonal band problems with Alschvitz, so John Lieb, an old Vats-rat friend of ours, played drums and eventually toured Europe with us. John also played in an early hardcore band, the Sluglords. He's currently with the Extra Action Marching Band, this far-out project that blows minds with its signature marching band on acid, punk meets circus, Sousa-like musical joy, put together by Simon Cheffins of Crash Worship. I personally love this band, and we got to hang out in recent years when we played together in Nijmegen, Netherlands.

Back in San Francisco, we settled in by getting back on food stamps and General Assistance, hanging with old friends, and telling stories from the Rock Against Reagan tour, the Canadian bust, and the many great gigs, bands, and people. I look at it all now, more than three decades later, and my mind boggles.

At home, I was really enjoying taking it easy and moving slow, when I got a call from Wouter Van De Brug, BGK's manager. He had a plan for flying MDC to Europe to play one last big show at Wyers Squat in Amsterdam, a public space forged from unused private space that courts had ruled must go back to the private owners for their personal use. Wouter also booked us with BGK for ten shows, mostly in the Netherlands, but with a few German shows and a Copenhagen, Denmark show on New Year's Eve.

No more kicking back and patching our bones. We had to prep for a winter tour. As someone once said, "You can sleep when you're dead."

Before we went to Europe, we had a charged up, down-home SF-style free daytime outdoor event in the Mission on October 23, 1983, playing the last Rock Against Reagan show for the year, which was a humdinger. Activist Dennis Peron put on the show. Whoopi Goldberg and Bobcat Goldthwait were the MCs, and the lineup consisted of Dead Kennedys, Contractions, and MDC. The show happened at Dolores Park at 18th and Dolores, a great place for a 10,000-person gig attended by a big crowd of San Franciscan punk, rainbow, gay, hipster, and bebop folks. Whoopee handled the mob with finesse on a beautiful autumn Bay Area day, one of my two or three favorite gigs of all time. If you had to live your whole life in one city (with rent control), it should be San Francisco, in one neighborhood, the Mission.

Second European Tour, 1983-84

We stayed in touch with Wouter, and it all was coming together. While finessing the logistics of getting to Europe at the last minute, we got in touch with Crass, and they were ready to help. A gig was planned in the UK just a few days before the Wyers / Amsterdam show. So we hurriedly flew into London. Lacking "working papers" (punk rock, right?), we tried to wing it: bad move.

Customs hauled us from the main room to a very Orwellian room with little glass booths. We overheard the British customs people mumbling about "the thousands of dead policemen band." They decided to refuse us entry and wanted to send us back on the next plane going to America. Bummer. Luckily, we got Wouter on the phone, and he insisted to British Immigration we had important government shows to do in the Netherlands. Suddenly, the Brits just released us. We had to buy five tickets with a credit card and immediately leave London for Amsterdam – many thanks to our then-roadie and all-around cool guy, Chris Charucki, and his brother, Rich, who lent his credit card to Chris for emergencies. But, sadly, we missed our gig with Crass. A potential piece of our history was silenced before it could be screamed, but the tour had to go on. British immigration escorted us to a KLM flight, and we flew off to Amsterdam.

We arrived in Amsterdam, and I could feel the excitement our hosts and punks in general were feeling. People felt a lot of sentiment for

Wyers Squat. Yet, the courts ruled against the squatters. For me, it was like playing a wake, but the crowd poured tons of love on us. We played with Pandemonium, a tight thrash unit from Venlo, Netherlands.

Everywhere we went, the Dutch people treated us well. The squat scene in Europe was in full bloom, too. One could say it was a golden age, and our brand of political hardcore matched up very well with that movement and lifestyle. Everyone wanted to chat us up, and we gladly received the attention, which felt good, considering local music writers in Austin once ranked us the 12th best punk band and went out of their way to call us a loser/nowhere band. In that small, Southern town, we broke tradition and skipped or cut our way to the head of the class. In the Netherlands, we were a million miles from that mentality. MDC represented American hardcore on stage and in the street. Our star was rising.

Holland is a part of the Netherlands that broke away from Spain in the 1500s. They were under the protectorate of Spain by some past historical treaty. This was the 16th century, and vast wars were taking place across Europe, including Catholic versus Protestant. Holland was becoming increasingly Protestant, intellectually freethinking, and socially tolerant. They accepted people's differences. This has continued to this day. Roughly, Holland is the more urban liberal part of the Netherlands, and it is often confused as being synonymous with all of the Netherlands. So don't let metonymy fuck with you.

As other artists/musicians will tell you, Germans treat bands very well, so being well-appreciated in places that don't speak English as a first language feels miraculous. The Berlin of 1983 was different than post-2000 Berlin: things really changed after the Wall came down; people were more relaxed all around. Between Germany, Austria, and Switzerland live over 100 million German speakers. I used to joke that life was too short to learn German. That, I learned, was poppycock. Germany is the center of punk rock on the continent so learning German is a cool, smart thing if you're staying in Europe for any amount of time.

Finally, we played Copenhagen, Denmark, a special lifelong dream because we rocked children of the Vikings. They, in turn, took us to Christiania, the largest squat in Europe featuring hundreds of people, its own cafes, restaurants, bookstores, hash shops, radio stations, and a post office. People had an alternative economy and lived their own way outside the mainstream. A lot of that has ended, but squatting's continued on, especially in Germany. These squats were so happening and a joy to play all over Europe. The BZ-brigaden from Copenhagen became two lifelong friends I totally adore, named Ulla Kopycinski and Karen Jorgensen. We hung with the Bz'ers and felt like distant warm family.

Soon we headed back to Amsterdam to catch a plane home, and to hear if our contacts had phoned us from Italy and Spain. We had been putting out teelers to them, and they had been communicating back enthusiastically. Instead of heading home, we planned a seven-week-plus tour lasting until the end of February. We were rolling, rolling, rolling... keep those Dead Cops rolling...

Europe did not let us go home. We got back to Amsterdam and received a call from Sid from Cheetah Chrome Motherfuckers, who said we could come down and play five or six shows around Italy with a bevy of bands. We decided immediately to figure out the logistics. Fortunately, we met an American fellow named Jay Fish, originally from California, who starting showing up at our shows, and had a small bankroll and was ready to back us with gas. The rest of the plan was to eat peanut butter and jelly sandwiches, and pasta with the locals. At the same time, Wouter was investigating gigs in Spain, and a nationally aired TV performance in Madrid seemed to be a possibility as well, at a Basque squat gig in northern Spain. This was so exciting — the Millions of Dead Cops Italia/Spain '84 tour.

Our crew at this point included me, Ron, Franco, and John (the players) with Chris Charucki, Tammy Lundy (our manager), Jay

Fish, and Wouter as tour manager. We repeated playing Hengalo and Groningen of the Netherlands, and then we aimed for Freiberg, West Germany, a quaint little city on the edge of the Black Forest. We played a cool little squat house called the A to Z, where we met Frank Berlin who became a lifelong friend. He studied master's level subjects concerning the German psyche following World War II, and proposed the Germans gave up their soul and sense of humor after their collective acknowledgement of the Master Race scheming: the vile hatred of the Jewish race, a race that had become integrated into German culture for nearly two millennium. Very fascinating stuff.

We drove from Germany through Switzerland, over and through the Alps, to Milan, or Milano, as it's called by Italians, and the famous Virus Squat. By the way, cities in Europe have two real names: one in English and the other in native tongues. So if you travel to Roma, then you refer to it in English as Rome, Vienna is Wien, and Cologne is Koln. Nobody told me this for many tours, so maybe I'll be the first one to share this with you.

Virus Squat, our first gig, happened at a courtyard house and meeting hall with a big stage surrounded by a wall. DIY American hardcore swelled into Italy. Everyone was smiling, so it was joyful, playful and memorable. We played with Impact, Wretched, Negazione, Contrazione, Kollettivo, Contropotere, and Jaggernaut, but the band that stood out the most was Cheetah Chrome Motherfuckers. They were up, down, and all around. They were straight up hardcore, but with a Crucifucksian sense of emergency.

Singing fully in Italian like a Fellini movie at high speed, they were really entertaining, charming, and even beautiful. We played Torino (home of Fiat), Ferrara (smaller city state town), Bologna (old-school working class center), and Milano (power center/business center of northern Italy). The food was delicious: real, fresh-made pasta with various marinara sauces. It's like Mexican food in San Francisco's Mission: every mamacita has her own style and taste. I soon found that if I spoke my Spanish 101 with an Italian accent, people would giggle but they usually could direct me to my needs and sometimes converse.

You can see how emotionally engaged everyone is here, quite different from the chillier, more detached way of doing things in northern Europe.

There is nothing like walking through Rome checking out the Pantheon (Temple of the Gods), ambling along the narrow streets with their three thousand years of artifacts. Centuries of people come and then they go. Also, if you're near Florence, stop in and see Donatello's statue, David. That piece of art kicked off the Renaissance with Donatello depicting David nude, leaving no doubt about his fruitful genitalia for all to see. In fact, a great book to get is Rick Steves' *Europe 101: History and Art for the Traveler*. It delineates different periods and styles of art and really helps identify eras. It enriched my European art experiences. Being part Italian, I totally related to and loved Italy. This tour started a long beautiful relationship between MDC and Italy with classic great shows spanning the course of three decades. Viva Italia!

Saying "Arrivederci" to Italy was sad, but our next adventure to Spain made us sit up. MDC was to be the first American band to tour Spain, which in 1983 was still old-fashioned, Francisco Franco-plundered Spain. Though the former died in 1975, the state apparatus and institutions remained, and paramilitary police forces roamed about the land doing whatever they wanted. They were all over the highways with checkpoints. When we got pulled over, Franco (our Franco, not the fascist dictator), who was always holding stashes of pot or hash, looked at me, like, "Holy shit, what do I do?" But he thought fast: he grabbed a bag of red pepper flakes, dumped the hash into it, and threw it in the food box. The Guardia Civil were the ones with the funny Mickey Mouse ears who were rough, no-fun, old-school fascist police. They looked at our passports like we were criminals, then they grunted and pointed and shouted for us to move as they searched our pockets. Next, they took out the police dogs that combed over our van. We were as scared as can be waiting to see if the dog in the back of the van was gonna find it. The dog went up to the red pepper three times, sniffed at it, but then sneezed and ran away. At last, the dog just moved on. Moments later, they packed up and had moved on. Holy bejesus!

We drove forty miles to Barcelona, quite the historic city, for our gig in old downtown. Street paths were thin as three or four feet wide in the barrio. We played about a 300-person place that probably had 500 folks crammed in. People were so hungry to feel it, dance to it, shout, and scream. With Franco and Ron, we could converse in Spanish to the crowd, and people loved that, but they were frozen in place trying to make sense of a style of music they weren't used to. It was an old school, no stage, in-their-face gig. Still, people were unsure. Nobody left, but a lot of puzzled looks filled the room. A few people talked to us, but people weren't sure how they ultimately felt. The next night we played again; it looked like the same exact crowd. Everyone was in place, standing, waiting, but this time from the very first note to the last they went absolutely apeshit bonkers, like we were returning conquerors.

The next night we played Zaragoza, a hip, working class town, and everyone loved it from the start. The night after that, we appeared on National Television in Madrid with a multi-thousand person crowd. We lip-synched part of our set for the cameras. Despite such fakery, I was glad to see this country growing up and growing out from under Franco's fascist rule. Check out the Museo Nacional Del Prado. That is the Metropolitan Museum of Art of Spain and it has much to offer, such as visiting Picasso's house and Dali's castle over towards Barcelona. Enjoy it and leave the running of the bulls to the idiots.

Our stay in Spain lasted only four crazily intense days before gigs in Germany, Denmark, and Holland. We stopped back at the well-known Korn-Strasse squat, then headed back into Berlin for a couple of shows, one at the KuKuk, where we ran into our old-time Berlin punk friend, Schnoorer, and one at the Front Kino. At the KuKuk, we played on the second floor at the end of a long narrow gangway. Eight cops came walking up on this ramp to tell me the gig was over. When the first one came near enough to me, because I was up above him, I swiped out and snatched the hat off his head, and the crowd went wild. I passed the hat around, and it was a comical scene to see the police retreat. It was almost like the Keystone Cops, and I got to be Charlie Chaplin.

After the Front Kino show, a place we've played many times through the years, we spent three days back in Copenhagen playing the now-torn down Ungdomshuset ("Youth House"), and we played Christiania and hung at their radio station as well.

Finally, we made it to our European home, Holland, and played a few shows with Crucifix and our buddies, No Pigs, from Amsterdam. Some Dutch skins tried to fuck with me in Lelystad, and it didn't go over well with my No Pigs, so the skins got straightened out. Despite the great experience, we endured homesickness and tiredness.

Dorothy wanted to click her heels and head home...

Dec 17– Amsterdam, Holland: Wyers: MDC + Pandemonium

Dec 18 – Groningen, Holland: Vera: MDC + BGK

Dec 20 – Amsterdam, Holland: Wyers: MDC + Base Jones

Dec 21 – Antwerp, Belgium/Paradox: MDC + Zyklome A + Moral Demolition

Dec 23 – Uithoorn, Holland/Shiva: MDC + BGK

Dec 24 – Hengelo, Holland/Babylon: MDC + BGK

Dec 25 – Venlo, Holland/Bauplatz: MDC + SCA (Staphorster Chaoten Alliante)

Dec 26 – Steenwijk, Holland/Buze: MDC + BGK + Local Disturbance + Boegies

Dec 28 – Hannover, Germany/Kornstraße: MDC + BGK + RAF Punk

Dec 30 – Copenhagen, Denmark/Saltlageret: MDC + BGK + City X

Dec 31 – Copenhagen, Denmark/BZ Brigaden Ryesgade 58: MDC

1984

Jan 2 – Copenhagen, Denmark/Youth Center Ungdomshuset Jagtvej 69: MDC

Jan 6 – Amsterdam, Holland/Wyers: MDC + ZX (Benefit to pay the electric bill)

Jan 14 – Hengelo, Holland/Babylon: MDC + No Pigs

Jan 15 – Groningen, Holland/Vera: MDC

Jan 20 – Freiburg, Germany/Anarchy Squat: MDC + Hawaii Five-O

Jan 21 – Freiburg, Germany/Anarchy Squat: MDC

Jan 27 – Milano, Italy/Virus - Via Correggio 18: MDC + Impact + Wretched

Jan 28 – Torino, Italy/Centri d'Incontro: Peggio Punx + Negazione + Contropotere + MDC + Contrazione + Kollettivo

Feb 2 – Ferrara, Italy: MDC + Juggernaut

Feb 3 – Bologna, Italy: MDC + Irha + Cheetah Chrome Motherfuckers

Feb 4 – Milano, Italy /Virus: MDC

Feb 6 – Barcelona, Spain/Zeleste: MDC

Feb 7 – Barcelona, Spain/Zeleste: MDC + Kangrena

Feb 9 – Zaragoza, Spain: MDC + Cuarto Reich

Feb 10 – Madrid, Spain/Sala Imperio: MDC.+ Interterror (broadcast national TV)

Feb 15 – Hannover, Germany/Kornstraße: MDC + Boskops

Feb 16 – Berlin, Germany/KuKuk: MDC + Porno Patrol

Feb 18 – Berlin, Germany/Front Kino: MDC + Razia + Boskops

Feb 21 – Copenhagen, Denmark/Youth Center Ungdomshuset Jagtvej 69: MDC + Negative IQ

Feb 22 – Copenhagen, Denmark/Christiania Lopen: MDC + Far Out

Feb 23 – Bremen, Germany: MDC

Feb 24 – Wielingen: Amsterdam, Holland: BGK + Crucifix + No Pigs + MDC

Feb 25 – Lelystad, Holland/De Roggel: MDC + Crucifix + BGK + Zyklome A + Blitzkrieg

Feb 26 – Venlo, Holland/Bauplatz: MDC + Crucifix + Incest

Home on the Range

This is a hard part of the book for me to write. I watched as a great lineup of MDC began to combust in slow motion. We arrived home, and everything was thrown upside down in our world. No funny little ironies help explain – we were four people that spent three years together, and Ron wanted out. Al was doing drugs like they were going out of style. John went back to the Sluglords. Yet, MDC had the "Chicken Squawk" EP to record. I started working on the 52 bands from around the world PEACE compilation with Franco. Ron received some money, so he decided start a business named Concrete Jungle, an ahead-of-its-time skateboard shop. We recorded "Chicken Squawk" and prepared for the last Rock Against Reagan show on July 4th in front of the Moscone Center in San Francisco, where the Democratic Convention was to take place. My band was calling July 4th our last show, but I was against all that.

July 4, 1984 was a sweltering day in San Francisco. Big protests had happened around the city for weeks. Mayor Dianne "Swinestein" Feinstein had been promising the press she wouldn't let the city be taken over by hooligans. Political actions in the form of die-ins were taking place at various financial buildings, including in front of the Bank of America headquarters. People held sit-ins at large intersections. Rock Against Reagan was going on at the stage across from the Moscone

Center, where the Dems were nominating presidential candidate Walter Mondale. The lineup for the day included Reagan Youth, DRI, the Dicks, MDC, Michelle Shocked, and the Dead Kennedys. People were coming in and hanging out between going and joining other demonstrations. The SF police were parading in packs of a dozen. Mounted police trotted nearby on horseback. Another thirty were tooling around on mini-motorcycles, driving in circles. Watching it all felt surreal. "Swinestein" promised San Francisco would not fall to "the kooks" and would not become "Kook City," which I thought was a good new name, or at least a new decent nickname, for our home city.

We got to the stage about noon and loaded in our gear. Some friends were heading off to a demonstration. First, though, we had to set up and do a sound check. I thought that it was gonna be a light show attendance-wise, but people started showing up in large numbers. About five thousand came that beautiful sunny afternoon. David of Reagan Youth was great. He did a version of "War Pigs" by Black Sabbath, and it was way cool. DRI did one of those 44 songs in 32-minute sets: an intense performance. They were tight, on their game, and smooth.

The Dicks played "No Fuckin' War" and had the whole crowd singing in the chorus. Our set, MDC, I'm not so clear about. Ron announced this was his last live gig. Al had separated himself from the band. He was definitely doing hard drugs, and it ruined our ability to relate to him. It really sucked. We should have just moved on and gotten another drummer. It didn't seem that easy to me because of our long friendship, but looking back, I should have made that move.

Some folk performers played, and I believe Michelle Shocked was on stage, but I got distracted after our set. I drifted off to the SF Police headquarters where a bunch of us were going to do a sit-in against the mass arrests that had started. About three hundred of us gathered and confronted a hundred cops, a dozen or so on horses, and about another thirty cops on the small motorcycles. These guys didn't wear uniforms. They had a sinister air about them.

So we set up at the corner, past the entrance to their HQ, and sat in the street. Our numbers drained down to about 200. The horses lined up like Cossacks in a row. Their tactic was to charge us: ride into and over us. Then the motorcycle cops rode in circles over us, hitting us, and ramming us over and over. I was holding the hand of a little gal named Jorin. She was struck by the charging horse's legs, and her jaw broke right in front of me. It was horrible how the mayor and the powers that be took their power and unleashed such brutality.

We really do live in the land of the Multi Death Corporation where Millions of Dead Cops will try to hurt and maim you. I wish you well, Jorin. This was one of the last demonstrations I went to for a while. The police had a picture of me torching some dumpster. I thought about this hard and concluded it was time to cool down, it was time to hide out and stay out of the public's eye. Two years melted away before our next MDC show. I hate when any of my MDC line-ups break up. It does not feel good.

You're Our Commie Fag

Back in San Francisco, early on, around 1982, I got to know some people who became the SF Skins, a street crew that used to hang out in the Haight. I'm talking about Mark Dagger, Beau, Bags, and Sonny. They lived the street life, as did MDC. They were certainly rough around the edges, could do some fucked-up shit, but they also protected the scene in their own way from rednecks and ultra-violent ghetto types who preyed on teenage runaways and thought street punk should be eradicated. We dealt with each other well enough, I suppose, but I'd always hear some hard-ass stories, so I can't stand behind their whole thing. To their credit, I hear they ripped off some pretty ugly people, but that's if you use the logic that somehow two wrongs can equal a right. I operated The Veggie snack bar, a small sandwich shop in the Mission district, and the SF Skins frequently came in ten minutes before closing time, checked how I was doing, and I generally handed out peanut butter and jelly sandwiches to the guys.

Late in the summer of '84, I was at a Sunday matinee show that wasn't too well attended. A few of the part-time weekend SF Skins were hanging around and started "sieg heil-ing" in front of the Mabuhay Gardens' front door. I was like, "Really, guys, what is up?" People hated punks, and the Chicano gangs would certainly be willing to fight. As I confronted the skins, a Chicano guy wearing a blue bandana and flannel shirt walked by and checked us out intensely. The skins sieg heil-ed again. I told them "to give it a damn break." The Chicano fellow in colors walked away, and the skins and I stood there. I asked, "Where are we going with all this? You guys aren't national socialists. You guys like the Dicks." In a flash, a Chicano gang of six comes tearing out of nowhere, knives drawn. A melee ensued, two of the skins got stabbed. I was up against a wall, knife pressed to my throat, and the original Chicano from earlier looked at me, looked at the guy with the knife, shook his head no, the knife left my throat, and they all just piled into a 1960s Chevy and were gone. I think all of us witnesses were in shock. I certainly was shaken up. An ambulance arrived. Two of the skins suffered nasty stabs and lacerations, but no one died.

I went home, and the next day I got a call from Angie Mima, a good old friend of mine. She said the SF Skins were looking for me, and they had fire in their eyes. "Be careful and be prepared," she advised, and I did for the next week or so.

I was living with my girlfriend, Jenny Jo Brown, her child, Rosel, and our son, Jesse, who was born in the summer in 1984. Then the rumor came down that some out-of-town skins were talking about setting fire to my place. Oh, boy. I realized I had to go up to the Haight and face the music. I told them I'd be there that evening at 7 p.m. in front of the pizza parlor at Masonic. I sent word in a note that I would take a beat-down, but leave my girlfriend and the kids out of it.

Off I went at the designated hour. There they were. I greeted them and asked they allow me to say three things. They agreed. First, I said that they must know that I was in no way connected to the guys in the Chicano gang, and I was as horrified as anybody about what went down.

"Okay, what else?" they asked.

I said, "I'm a commie fag of sorts, and I'm always gonna say something when you're sieg heil-ing in front of the punk club. It's in my DNA to say shit. I mean, read the band's lyric sheets. I don't like Nazi Socialism."

Lastly I said, "I brought $30, and I'd rather get drunk with you than get my ass kicked."

They all looked at each other, and I believe it was Mark Dagger who put me in a headlock and said, "You do act like a commie fag,

Dave, but at least you're *our* commie fag. Now, let's go drink."

Off drinking we went. We inspected the stab wounds and commiserated about it all. What did I learn? At the least, I know whose commie fag I am.

The Best Dog I Never Wanted

They say you're either a dog person or a cat person. I used to think I leaned towards being a dog person, but as an adult I never have owned a cat or a dog until lately, when I have been adopted by many feral cats. I like the low maintenance aspect of a cat, and being on the road for periods of time seems less hard on my cats.

Anyway, 1985, in San Francisco, I was living with my girlfriend, Jen, and our son, Jesse, and my stepdaughter, Rose. We lived in the Rat House, a skinny flat at the corner of 16ᵗʰ Street and Landers on the edge of the Mission and Castro neighborhoods, which evolved into a focal point with roommates doing zines, playing music, and throwing parties. Ray Melville, Joe Britz who owned the actual pet rat and started the Rat House zine, Lawrence Livermore of Lookout Records, Lil Mike of the Bedlam Rovers, and Debbie Stockman were among the dozens of housemates for the ten years it lasted. It wasn't quite what the Vats had been, but it served as MDC headquarters and was a free hostel for many a visitor.

But when this story took place, our little family of four shared a tiny room, but that didn't stop Jen from announcing that she had told a stranger she met at the food-stamp office that we would watch his dog, named Alex, while he entered a rehab clinic for the next ninety days. I knew where this was going, so immediately told Jen that she was going to walk the dog and do all the other chores related to keeping a dog.

With that said, I resigned myself to pretty much being responsible for the dog.

There we resided that winter, as snug as you can be with fleas on an often-soiled rug, all of us in a 12' x 14' room. The dog, a Great Dane, was a look-alike for Scooby Doo with none of the charm. He was as big as a pony. He was of a fair nature, but rather oblivious to humans unless you had food. He was a big drooler, he smelled, and tended to have bad gas. He would lean up against the window, survey the scene, and if he spotted a cat or another dog he would go nuts. All of a sudden nothing would matter except getting at that other animal. When walking him, you had to be ever vigilant to spot the other animal first to prepare for this forward surge of arm-wrenching power. This was quite like the end credits of *The Jetsons* when Astro jerks George out of his post-modern conveyer-chair.

On more than one occasion, Alex would react to a startling sound so violently and instinctively that if one of the kids had been in the wrong place, at the wrong time, they could have been severely injured. I mentioned this to Jen with a tone of self-righteousness and saw by her demure response that she agreed, so I didn't dwell. We were in the last days of the last month we would have Alex. Our tiny apartment would be Alex-less once again. That Sunday there was a street fair up in the Haight. Jen suggested I get Alex out of the house, and soon we were big stepping up into Haight-Ashbury.

The hardcore punk scene had experienced a lot of trauma in the previous few years. In 1980-81, the national scene became aware of how widespread and how cool it was, including different punk scenes in New York, Boston, LA, Washington DC, San Fran, Austin, Houston, Reno, Akron, East Lansing, Detroit, Montreal, and on and on. Then, somewhere in 1983-84, we realized how different we were: Bad Brains, the Misfits, Agnostic Front, the Meatmen, and MDC had a lot less in common with each other than we all had thought. A backlash against *Maximum Rocknroll*, the West Coast magazine with its left-wing slant, was in full swing. It was denounced as a preachy punk rock rulebook. MDC were the darlings of the left-wing scene. A lot of skinheads took this anti-left wing view some very radical steps farther afield. They began to make some very real connections with white supremacists and started out-and-out attacking our scene, as well as racial minorities and gay people.

One skinhead named Terry Nohawk, formerly known as Terry Mohawk, started making threatening overtures towards me. I didn't take it personally because we had been old scene people and generally those folks, no matter how right-wing they were, respected the fact we'd been in the scene together for years. I should have known, for some folks, this doesn't mean a thing.

At the corner of Haight and Belvedere, Nohawk and another thug started yelling at me. Slowly they walked towards me, menace in their eyes, faces filled with twisted anger as they both raised their blackjack-like weapons. I braced myself, wondered if anyone was witnessing this nightmare in progress, and then I saw the most wonderful sight. My canine companion jumped up, straddled Terry's head, and rapid-fire bit that crazed Nazi all about the face. Then, a moment later, Alex was up again, gnawing on Terry's companion's leg. It was beautiful seeing them retreat, cry, curse, and vow revenge while fleeing as I tightly held the leash of the beast and said, "Good boy, Alex! Good boy!"

This long-time vegetarian bought a raw steak for Alex that night. And I guess for that next week or so, I felt like kind of a dog person. A week later, Alex's owner showed up at our door. I very sadly let Alex go. I just hope he had a good life.

The Gordon Fraser Days

Between late 1984 to '86, MDC didn't seem to go anywhere. The hole Ron left in the band was pretty massive. I've never been able to just put an ad in a paper or even post a flyer for a musician. I wanted it to be organic. That, I guess, was a lot to ask. We implored a few guitar-playing friends, but no one even wanted to try. Alschvitz, Franco, and I would show up to practice and play as a three-piece over and over. Nobody, and I mean *nobody*, wanted me to pick up the guitar. I'm a guitar strummer and wrote a lot of songs for MDC, but I'm in no way a double-stroking, power chord, rhythm machine working on the level where Ron Posner set the bar. We didn't know where to turn.

One night we started hearing this lead guitar wailing away somewhere in the building where we practiced. At times, it sounded like Eric Clapton, at other times like Stevie Ray Vaughan. It was so bluesy. We stood outside the door and listened and listened, and finally knocked. An unassuming guy, named Gordon Fraser, opened the door, and we asked if he wanted to jam. He kind of looked behind himself as if he couldn't believe we were talking to him.

We finally were able to get him in our practice room, and within a little while we were playing "Politician" by Cream. Al and I were total Cream-heads from the late '60s. We then played "Born Under a Bad Sign," and Gordon could certainly wail. Then we told Gordon about MDC, and we played him "Corporate Death Burger." He didn't have the double-stroking finesse of Ron, but he could reach back and deliver a lead. We went through songs, and without a doubt, he could play. We noticed right away that Gordon was one of the shyest individuals that we had ever met. He didn't make a lot of eye contact, and he was very soft-spoken.

Our first point of business was finishing up what was to become the *Smoke Signals* album that John Marquand did the art and layout for. We got into the studio and finished up quickly. We wanted to get it out and do a tour. It was an odd album with a little of this and a little of that, recorded piecemeal at various times over the course of a year. I liked some of the songs but it was haphazardly put together, although "No More Cops" remains in our set to this day. But at least we had a touring unit. After our long absence from playing out, it felt good. We gigged at the Farm in SF with Youth of Today, Cheetah Chrome Motherfuckers, and BGK, and it was nice to rock the town again.

We then set out on an 18-city tour to the Midwest and East Coast, the highlight of which was playing with DOA featuring Jello Biafra on vocals, Celtic Frost, Samhain, and Cheetah Chrome Motherfuckers for the New York Music Festival at the Ritz in NYC.

After NYC, on the way back to the West Coast, during the Midwest leg of the tour, we got pulled over by the police in Zanesville, Ohio. The cops thought we were some kind of drug dealers because we looked sketchy to the good people running the local Holiday Inn (this was the first and last Holiday Inn we ever stayed at). Franco had a satchel of various herbs – sage and herbs to burn in the hotel room to help him relax while he was meditating or doing yoga – as well as 20 hits of blotter LSD. He immediately ate the acid and tried to hide the herb packages – there was no pot because we had smoked it all – the cops pulled us out of the van, searched it, found Franco's herbs and thought it was marijuana, and arrested Franco. My friend, Mark Dubicki, who was a roadie for us on the tour, seriously explained to the Zanesville police that Millions of Dead Cops was really pro-police and sympathized with the plight of police, and we actually felt bad about all the millions of dead cops. Nevertheless the police held Franco for 72 hours, and we contacted a lawyer, explaining to everyone that they were just herbs, not pot. The cops checked his poop because they were sure he had ingested something. Franco said he had a wild electric ride in the jail there. After 72 hours, the police were forced to release him and he was still kind of glowing. And so we continued with our tour there in 1986. We lost three nights of gigs because of this nonsense, which sucked.

Back home, we worked on the *Millions of Damn Christians* album and had a much better time with the music we put together from scratch. Tom Flynn of Boner Records (who also started the band Fang) backed us, so we had a label we could call home. We released the album in 1987. On the album cover, we dressed in apostles' garb and sat with Jesus at the Last Supper. Christian groups condemned it, and people placed us on lists with Slayer as one of the most evil bands in America. That really helped album sales.

We got the *Millions of Damn Christians* album released in Europe on We Bite Records and toured Europe, focusing heavily on Germany and England. We played with Napalm Death in London and stayed in Germany for a month of gigs.

One night during this month-long stay in Germany, I met this beautiful young German woman with the greenest, most hazel eyes I had ever seen. It took me a bit of time to warm up, but after a while I had this shy, quiet, very attractive woman smiling at my charm. Eagerly, she listened to the story of my real passion in this life: surfing and my worldwide search for the perfect wave. At one point, she excused herself, got up, and went to the bathroom. I was sitting there feeling very highly of myself, thinking how far I'd come. I remembered how back in high school pretty women like these wouldn't ask me for the time, nevertheless sit, converse, and beg my pardon to use the bathroom. Yes, a very long way, I reminded myself. And then another woman tapped me on my shoulder and said, "My name is Olga, and Ute is my best friend. You better not fuck with her or I'll have to deal with her!"

I said, "What, I wouldn't dream of it."

She said, "Good, she is going through some terrible times and doesn't need some American asshole to fuck with her head. Her grandmother is very sick and the government has cut off her welfare and you better not mess with her."

I nodded, and said, "Okay," and when she returned I felt a wee bit sobered up. We started talking again, and I directed the conversation toward her life and asked how she was doing? She talked a little bit, her eyes drifted out into space, and I could see them welling up with tears. *Oh my,* I thought and touched her hand.

I imagined myself being Humphrey Bogart comforting Ingrid Bergman in *Casablanca*. I was the self-confident American male, reaching out to my hurting European female counterpart. I reached into my pocket and handed her two hundred Deutschmarks and said, "I heard some stuff," and told her I wanted her to have the money and to use it to go see her grandmother." She got up, said she'd be right back, and I saw her and her friend leave. I thought about it all as I nursed my scotch on the rocks, my drink of choice back then. I was feeling very stoic. I might exaggerate a story or two, but underneath it all, I was a good person.

This thought held for quite a bit until the bartender came up to me at the bar and said, "Hey, surfer Joe, don't worry too hard about Ute. She and Olga work all you American dudes." At first, it seemed so wrong, but after a little thinking on it I concluded, what goes around indeed does come around.

Something that became apparent as we went along was that Gordon wasn't enjoying the tour. He would isolate himself and cling to his guitar like a security blanket on the long van rides. He became withdrawn although he was still able to play hard on stage. I asked him if there was anything I could do, and he said to get him home as soon as possible. We had an opportunity to stay and do a few extra gigs, but the band knew to just get home. Our Amsterdam Van Hall gig was one of the last ones we did with Gordon.

Bad Moon at Gilman & the Pope Visits SF

MDC played 924 Gilman Street in Berkeley with Operation Ivy and Gang Green in May 1987, a typical night at Gilman, except rumors surfaced that a white-power, Aryan skin community had set up somewhere in North Bay. Showing up every now and again at Gilman for the preceding few months were 35 to 40 of their goons. Initially, they contented themselves by jumping people away from the club which sucked but eventually they got emboldened and had started coming up to the door. I wasn't really up on it, like Orlando X (Orlando Xavier) and Fraggle (Mark Martone), the bouncers at Gilman Street. They were trying to keep the masses safe and knew what was going on.

I lived in the West Bay and was a part-timer, at best, in the East Bay scene. But really, I didn't need to live in the East Bay to see forty guys with clubs and baseball bats were heading directly to the club without anything in between. I looked at the ten-person crew working security and said, "Fuck, it's just us," and "Hey, I'm a lover, not a fighter." Anyway, combat commenced. The skinheads' battle plan was to split into six groups of six and come at us staggered. It didn't make any sense because their overwhelming force was diminished. We got to menace them with equal numbers, then turn around and deal with the group behind us.

Holy baseball bats, Robin! Damn, like *West Side Story*, like *The Warriors*, we just kept clashing for what felt like an hour. Orlando got his collarbone broken, others were clobbered hard, but like the Spartan 300, we held the line, and in the end they got in their ratty Suburbans and drove off. It was very crazy, so scary, way exhilarating, and my heart was pounding right out of my chest. Right after the battle it was time to get on stage and sing, but I was too numb to be able to change gears to talk about it from the stage. As I remember, we just plowed through the set. At the end of the night, we warriors just looked at each other. There was nothing to say but goodnight, and, "Orlando, get some ice on that."

RIP, Fraggle. What a good guy. We played his house parties over and over in Oakland through the years. He was a "give you the shirt off his back" punk. Please, Fraggle, do Rest in Peace. All you be careful and be well, too. Fraggle died of natural causes; no violence was involved.

In September 1987, Pope John Paul II came to visit San Francisco. The town was abuzz. He had his Popemobile, and he was touring the town along a planned route. San Francisco, surprisingly, was locked down in a joyous glee. The gay and political community was aware of what a right-wing zealot he was, but most people thought the Polish Pope was cute despite his anti-gay/anti-woman worldview. With our *Millions of Damn Christians* record recently released, we had the perfect unofficial soundtrack of the Pope's visit.

We learned the Pope would be visiting SF's original Catholic church, established by Spanish missionaries, the Mission Dolores Basilica on Dolores and 16th Street. I was living at 16th and Landers, mere feet from the path of the Pope's route. The idea of playing a song or two in earshot of the Pope seemed like something we absolutely had to do. Debra Stockman, Lydia Paweski, Ray Melville, Cammie Toloui, Janey Guzman, and a bunch of the *Maximum Rocknroll* shit workers came on down.

Our plan was pretty straightforward: hide the musical equipment, set up under a tarp, give ourselves haircuts like monks from the Middle Ages, wait for the right time to remove the tarp, and start playing as our friends took out banners announcing our performance: greeting the Pope and protesting the Catholic Church's stand on gays. Sure enough, the Popemobile rounded the corner, we ran out, removed the tarp, and launched into "Multi Death Corporation." You could see 200+ cops come swarming towards us from every direction. Next up was "This Blood's For You." The local police got to me first. They yelled, "Down on the ground," and I hit the deck with our crew. Next thing, I looked up and standing over us are dozens and dozens of cops, different types of police and sheriffs. One SF policeman asked me, "Do you want to learn how to fly?" and pointed off the edge of the roof.

"No, sir," I replied. Then the Secret Service whisked me away downstairs and into my apartment. At the same time, I noticed they were rude to the SF police, and it was obvious the SF police didn't like it. The Feds told the SF police that they would take it from here, and closed the door in Lieutenant O'Brien's face. They asked who was in charge, and I volunteered myself.

"Who are you?" asked Agent Dunkin. I could see his badge and nametag on his belt. "Well, I am David Dictor, sir. We are peace punks, and we are playing for the Holy Father, and we are just making a political statement."

"Why?" they wanted to know, and I went into my thoughts about John F. Kennedy's assassination and the downward spiral of America since then. He was Catholic and I was Catholic. We're talking Catholic brotherhood here, folks. In seconds, the Secret Service were packing up and racing out, and they told the SF police to do with us what they wanted. SF Police Lieutenant O'Brien looked at me and then at the room full of SF police, and said, "Well, we don't want him, or any of them," and just like that, all the police left. They dropped the musical equipment they started to impound on the fire escape steps. A few of the officers came over, shook my hand, and asked for a signed album. You make new fans where you can. It's funny, too, because a few of the cops wound up feeling like they knew me, and would honk and wave from their patrol cars in the future.

Metal Devil Cokes & Dead Cops Rock, 1988

With Gordon's retirement after the pope stunt, we were back to square one, but this time around, without delay, I bumped into an old friend, Eric Calhoun, who played for the band the Wolverines. I asked him if he had the time and the inclination to play with MDC. He felt inclined, temporarily. Right off, we sounded potent in the practice room. Before too long, we planned tours of North America. Jenny Jo Brown came up with the art for the Corporate Death Burger and Skateboard Jesus t-shirts. The highlight of touring that summer was playing the Anarchist Gathering in Toronto put on by activist Michael Smith (RIP), Robin Banks, and the Toronto anarchy crew.

That summer, Canadian authorities with nothing better to do were not letting young punky Americans into the country, so we were turned away at Niagara Falls. We called Michael Smith who invited us, and he directed us to a First Nations reservation on the Saint Lawrence Seaway. There we got out, checked in, and said we were friends of Michael Smith. The people at the desk said, "Well, that's nice," and let us stand there fifteen minutes more before asking if we would like to see their museum. We saw artifacts, models of villages from olden days, art and crafts, and animal hides. They guided us through the museum, and we just went along watching and asking a few questions. At the end of the tour, they asked if our van was locked and if we had everything. We said that our driver would stay with the van, and we were all good.

We were led down into a boat port and told to hop into this dinghy that was about twelve feet long. They told us to lie down and pulled a tarp over us. Within moments, we were motoring across the St. Lawrence River, and ten minutes later, we reached the Canadian side. The man who drove the boat said, "Get out and go straight up to the road, and, if you see a car with a siren, duck down, run, and forget what I look like." We jumped into the knee-high water and ran about two hundred yards up to the road where we found an old Chevy van with one Michael Smith behind the wheel.

"Get in quick," he yelled, and we were racing down the road. We got onto the highway and saw a sign that read, *Toronto 140 miles.*

We made it to the festival, took part in the workshops, and had a great time with our hosts. That night, we played early even though we were headlining, and just as we got off the stage there were a host of Canadian officials surrounding the band Scream's van looking for MDC. We slinked away on foot and went back to our host's place for the night. What an adventure we had.

Back in the day, Rebecca Tucker of the band Frightwig offered to make me some costumes to wear on stage: a Divine outfit and an Elvis outfit. I took her up on it, and when I got the Elvis oufit, I put it on and left it on. I wore it at home. I wore it to local gigs, and then on tour in 1988 I wore it every day, except when I was wearing the Divine outfit. Between our regular set, I'd play "Love Me Tender," "Don't Be Cruel," and a version of "Jail House Rock" renamed "Dead Cops Rock." We would go on tour, and I was a bit insufferable, sometimes playing "Love Me Tender" for an encore instead of "John Wayne Was A Nazi," or one of our other standbys.

I was doing my thing. One night we were playing Racine, Wisconsin, and the cops called off the show early for some noise ordinance bullshit and claimed the promoter hadn't scheduled the event correctly. So the lieutenant and the sergeant left one lone officer to clear us and about fifty kids out and get us on our way. As we loaded out the gear, I approached the officer and asked if he was an Elvis fan, and he told me, "Yes, I am, I loved the king." I offered to play one acoustic Elvis song right there on the side of the road, and the policeman said, "Okay, just one."

We played "Don't Be Cruel." The kids loved it, and the policeman tapped his nightstick along to the rhythm. Between the cop keeping time, Alschvitz playing his sticks on the street, and me, we were a rocking little threesome. Before we stopped, I just plowed into "Viva Las Vegas." Now, the policeman was shaking his hips and doing the twist. Everyone was shouting "Viva Las Vegas!" and it was pretty funny and we kept rocking.

The policeman was taking turns with me singing the lead. He was shouting and into it. Without stopping, I broke into "Love Me Tender." Everyone joined in. I slowed down the tempo, and everyone sang backup or hummed along. Just at that moment, the police car with the two superior officers returned and pulled up to the curb. The lieutenant growled, "O'Malley, what the fuck is going on!?"

We all looked at each other, and Alschvitz shouted, "Elvis is leaving the auditorium," as I hopped into our RV. Everyone cheered, the cop smiled, the crowd dispersed, and like that a beautiful moment was all over.

When I was touring in '88, I was also wearing my Divine drag outfit for about a third of our shows. The famous John Waters' film actor died in March 1988, and the name of this tour was Mourn Divine Correctly. It was a lot of fun, and we underlined our credentials as a gender-bending, whacked-out band. It was a great tour. We played with A.P.P.L.E. in NYC at Hell's Kitchen and with our buddies, the Witnesses.

Near the end of the tour, our guitar player, Eric, showed me how his hand was cramping up, and it was getting harder and harder to get through the set. Back in San Francisco, he was diagnosed with Carpal Tunnel Syndrome. After we finished our *Metal Devil Cokes* album, the lineup was kaput. Eric is a great guy and lives in the Northwest somewhere. He drops in on a gig about every two years.

Quick note: *Metal Devil Cokes* were words devised by Al's son, Brian Schultz, when he was about three years old; sarcastically, it represented three things destroying Amerikkka. Brian lives in Portland these days, is doing well, and occasionally roadies for present day MDC.

If I Had A Face Like Yours I'd Shave My Ass and Walk Backwards

Hey, Cop!!! If I Had a Face Like Yours… I'd Shave My Ass and Walk Backwards was our next album recorded with Al, Bill "the Cat" Collins of Fang and Special Forces fame, Matt Freeman of Operation Ivy, and myself. Bill really wanted to capture the ferocity of the first album, and I feel we did a steady job. We did a song called "Millions of Dead Cops" that wasn't hardcore, but it crunches hard; we did some fine work, my favorites being "Money Pile," "Beat Somebody Up," "The Crime of Rape," and "The Jew That Got Away," a song about my grandfather, Max Dictor, who got out of Germany before WWI and moved to Chicago. When we played the conservative parts of Bavaria, it was real different than Berlin or Hamburg, people would look at us, with our funny haircuts and all, and we'd get up on stage and play it to let them know we were aware of their history. We booked a tour and hit the road with Debbie Stockman, Al's son Brian, and Tim Armstrong as our roadie. We had a short school bus and off we went.

We played with Fugazi in Minneapolis. We played with Stza from Leftover Crack at the C Squat in NYC, we played with grindcore, hate core, crossover, emo bands, and the beginnings of melodicore. Around this time, Green Day was getting hugely popular. There were fewer and fewer hardcore bands. Tim Armstrong, Matt Freeman, and Al started playing Operation Ivy ska music while messing around before soundcheck, and people got off on it big-time. Still, MDC held its own in the changing music scene, but the times were a-changin' fast. A lot of hardcore bands threw in the towel. I myself started writing more straight-up punk songs. It was a different landscape out there.

Meanwhile, in 1990, a plot was hatched to kill me. Yes, me, David Dictor. I didn't know it then, and didn't know it until twenty years later in 2011. MDC was touring northern California, staying at Mikey Rat and Leasa Catera's place in Oakland, and here let me say, Mike and Leasa have let us crash at their pad time and time again. Putting up a band every now and then is noble. They are the most generous and friendly people you will ever meet, and have been that way from day one. It was during this four-day stay at their house when Mike Smith, MDC's bassist, and Russ Kalito, then our sometimes first, sometimes second, guitarist, went out to shoot pool at a local tavern. There they met these greasy, longhaired scuzz buckets. Prompted at the sight of an MDC t-shirt, one of the guys turned to Mike and decided to tell him an amusing anecdote.

Twenty years ago, he told Mike, he was offered $2,000 to rub me out. He waited, but the money never came, and the people who were going to hire him backed out of the deal. Mike and Russ were like, "What?!" and tried to drill him for more information. Later that night at the Verbal Abuse/MDC show at the Hazmat, a legendary warehouse space in Oakland, Mike saw the guy again, but he skipped off.

What are my thoughts? Well, this is the life we choose. There is no safety zone. Then, it's just, please don't do it! Shit, this is the world we live in. If being me is enough to warrant contracting an assassin to take me out, then I still got to be me. Suffice it to say, maybe it was good I was going to Europe.

Harley, John Joseph, and Me

Harley and John Joseph are the two main guys of the Cro-Mags.
I met them back in 1982. Both are rough and tumble guys with hard
edges. I met Harley in San Francisco when he was running with what
was to become the SF Skins. I met John Joseph for the first time when
he was standing down six guys, including Jimmy Gestapo. Those six
guys were backing the wrong guy, and John let them know they were
fucking with the wrong guy. He was very convincing. John is as hard as
nails, and I always liked him. Harley I liked too, but again I can't stand
behind all his acts, and there were some nasty acts on those hard streets
where street culture met gay culture met punk culture in the late 1970s
and early '80s.

Harley and I brushed up with each other through the years. One
time while playing Chicago he came up to me after our show and
asked if I could give him some money because the band had left him
behind and he was broke. I reached in my pocket and took out a fifty.
He nodded, said thanks, and was gone. I didn't see either of those folks
for five to six years. The Cro-Mags tore up Europe on their MAD tours.

Around 1990, I visited New York and saw that Cro-Mags were
supposed to play CBGB, so I ventured down to the club. I was standing
by the door when about eight skinheads in green flak jackets were
suddenly all right in front of me. They asked if I was who they thought
I was, and I said, "Hey, I probably am."

They all moved towards me, and I figured this was the big beat down I knew I was gonna get one day. I'd had one before in Santa Cruz, CA, when I tried to defend a guy from a cue-ball-headed mob of skinheads. It didn't go well but after my beating I managed to crawl on stage and perform for about fifteen minutes.

Anyway, these skins were certainly aiming to kick my ass but then Harley and John stood up, right there in front of me, and Harley said, "Are these assholes bothering you, Dave?"

Before I could say a word, John looked them over and said, "It's time for you fucking little girls to go back to Jersey."

They started whining, "Come on, Harley, we're buddies. What's it to you about protecting this asshole?"

John answered, "Mind your own business. It's time to head your asses back to Jersey," and that's what they did. Another bad pummeling averted. John walked away and Harley told me to enjoy the night.

With the same *Hey Cop!!!* line-up, we went to Europe, along with Bill's girlfriend, Aisha, for our All Roads Lead to Rome tour, where we started and ended the tour with a van driver/owner named Fitzjoy. We played Italy and Spain extensively, and did a show in Madrid for 2,000 people. We played Belgium, Holland, Croatia, and Germany. Venues were being run differently, though, particularly the squats. There was a big change in the scene between 1988 and 1993. Punk rock was bringing in money. Some squats were gouging bands. Bands figured if 500 people were coming to the show, and they charged the equivalent of $6 to get in, then where did the $3,000 go? The logic was that a band's payday should reflect the money brought in.

The rise of independent promoters steered bands away from the squats. It was good in one sense, for the payday of the bands, but ultimately the gigs took on more of a commercial feel, and that was really too bad and started a new trend in Europe. All of a sudden, door prices doubled, and a less egalitarian feel arose.

In Rome, this wasn't the trend yet. We played a great squat called Forte Prenestino, a fort and horse stable from the 1600s. You would pay the equivalent of a few dollars, be able to get a bowl of soup, watch a movie, throw pottery, and go outside and catch a band. We played for over a thousand people there. Terrific.

But that wasn't the trend in Germany. I tried to discuss with the squat promoters that they shouldn't put a $500 cap on touring bands because a band that flies to Europe needs to buy airfare, rent a van and equipment, feed itself, and pay rent at home, but they just couldn't see it. Both sides were destroying something precious we had created in the early and mid '80s. That was sad to see.

MDC went home and drifted our own ways. Bill was going to get married and move east. Matt always wanted to go back and team up with Tim again (they created Rancid). Al and I were back on our own, preparing for a very slow 1991. I went east to stay with my parents and was kind of shaken up by the changing scene. I wondered if we fit in any more and was getting tired of being in a political band that punk activists thought was earning too much money, while we felt we weren't making enough. The DIY early punk ethos seemed to be in flux, and I was ready to step back for a while.

Bill Collins, Matt Freeman, and Tim Armstrong are all really good people, and I am happy, proud, and grateful of their time in MDC.

M D C

SHADES OF BROWN

USA, Europe, and Russia, 1993

In 1993, MDC's touring lineup was Alschvitz, Chris Wilder, and Erica Liss for the *Shades of Brown* album. We booked ourselves some shows in Southern California, one of them at Club Costa Mesa. The show was in the afternoon, and we arrived a little late. Two bands had played already, and a band we knew a bit, Rigor Mortis, were just starting their set. I gave the place a quick once over and everything seemed just a little off: the beer signs, the furniture, and the outfits of some of the people. There were skinhead types around, but they were not vibing anyone. But something was wrong, I felt it.

Rigor Mortis finished their first song when one, then two, people started sieg heil-ing towards the bar. The bartender saluted back and then the Barbie barmaid did it. "Fuck 'Nazi Barbie'," I said. And then about twenty people were sieg heil-ing and about forty folks like us are just standing there. Rigor Mortis, having seen what I witnessed, made it a very short set. We were up next, so the MDC players huddled to discuss how to handle what was happening. Chris Wilder, about the best guy in the world, wanted to put it to them, rip them a new asshole. I countered that we were outnumbered and to please follow my lead.

About thirty people in the crowd stood right in front of us as we started the set, and about forty more stood further toward the back. I started talking generalities, "We're all the same here, and we are fighting for what we believe, and we believe the meat industry sucks, and this song is called 'Corporate Death Burger.'" And we played it hard, and it all went without a hitch. I guess everyone can get their head around "the starving children deserve a break today" line. But it was still strange, and then just like before, the whole place started sieg heiling: the skinheads, regular looking people, hell, 'Nazi Barbie', too. I had to put it out there and say something. I stated, "Sieg heil-ing is really not our thing, but we'll take it to mean 'I love you.' And thank you, for coming, this next song is 'Dead Cops.' "

Everybody loves "Dead Cops": fast, slick hardcore with biting lyrics. Everyone cheered, no sieg heil-ing erupted this time, so on we rolled. We played "Dick For Brains." Everyone digs an "I'm a sex addict" song. The crowd was all smiling: skinheads, Nazi Barbie, everyone, and we played "Chicken Squawk" and "My Family Is A Little Weird." Everyone was chill; there was no sieg heil-ing, and no fights. Time came to get out of there, short and sweet, and then I introduced "John Wayne Was A Nazi." The whole placed sieg heiled. I mean more than half of everybody. At this point, I state, "We so disagree, and you know it. You see me as some commie punk, and I guess to you, I am. But I want to break down the hate 'cause we are not so different, and hope we can learn to get along." Most people cheered for us, then sieg heiled, and we kicked out a hard, fast, "John Wayne," and that was that. We didn't have to fight our way out. It was a weird ass show.

In the summer of 1993, we were booked to play Seattle on our way to Europe and Russia. I was standing by the door of the Green Tortoise night club when an unshaven young man came up, shook my hand, and announced he was a fan of our music. Twenty minutes after he left, Chris Wilder, my guitarist at the time, told me that guy was Kurt Cobain and was surprised by how nonchalant I was being about our interaction. With this information, I went back out to look for Kurt but he was already gone. I would later find out that he had us on a list of his favorite albums of all-time where we placed #7 with our first album, *Millions of Dead Cops.*

In Europe, after leaving Stockholm and riding a cruise ship through the Scandinavian archipelago to the Finnish coast, Chris, Erica, Al and

I arrived in beautiful Turku, Finland. Visions of Vikings danced in my brain as I gazed at the chilly, star-filled sky.

When we reached the state-funded community culture house, the locals ushered us into a toasty back room and two blonde goddess-like maidens served up a delicious, heavily spiced onion-cabbage medley. After two large fragrant servings, I was stuffed silly like some childhood Thanksgiving memory, so I settled in for a short nap.

Suddenly, someone pounded frantically pounded at the door, pleading, "Please do your performance now," which jolted me from the hard sleep. Gas streamed from my mouth and bottom: the soup had me roiling…

Halfway through our set, my bowels were super-restless. Pain seared through me. Crossing my legs, I fought through "Damn Christians" and "This Blood's For You" before bolting through the crowd futilely towards the toilet... Before grasping the door, yes, I filled my pants.

Slowly, carefully, I walked to the toilet to clean up. Three young Finns followed me, exhorting me to play "John Wayne." They saw my predicament, and I'm sure they could smell it as well.

I cleaned up to the best of my abilities, considering the facility, then walked back on stage and confessed my accident to the crowd. Mercifully, most couldn't understand me. Then we unleashed the rest of our fiery set.

Indeed, one can shit oneself, both figuratively and literally. I am accomplished at both. Not proud of it. Just telling the truth. Living the *Shades of Brown* reality.

After the Scandinavia shows, MDC went to Russia with the *Shades of Brown* lineup. That's Chris Wilder, Erica Liss, Alschvitz, and myself. My friend, Candace Blankenship, came to film us, and Al's ten-year-old son, Brian Schultz, joined us as well. We had a splendid tour through Europe for a few months, saving our money for the Russian visas and other expected costs. We hooked up with Tribe 8, America's favorite queercore band, and we popped some eyes on that tour as we delivered something Europe needed to see: Tribe 8 vocalist Lynn Breedlove wearing a strap-on, inviting people to suck it while she sang.

Eventually, we would wind up in Copenhagen right before we were to drive across Sweden to catch a ferry to Finland and enter Russia.

Two days before we left for Russia from Copenhagen, the ruble dropped from three to the dollar to nine to the dollar, due to a Russian political crisis between President Boris Yeltsin and the military. Our Russian handlers held the tour hostage, demanding that we needed to come up with an additional $5,000 to make the tour happen. With nowhere to turn, I called Tim Yohannan. He came through with a $5,000 loan that he later forgave and it was handed over to our hosts to rent the halls, pay for our transportation, our protection, our accommodations, our food, and other costs.

Maybe we were extorted some, maybe a lot. I wouldn't be shocked. Anyway, we drove from Helsinki around the Baltic Sea on a lonely little road, and four hours later we arrived in St. Petersburg. We played an old communist hall to about 1,200 people, who totally went off, like they did the next night at the smaller Tom Tom Club, as they did at our Moscow MTV studio gig, as well as the Minsk, Belarus gig.

The last gig was in Kaliningrad, which is on the Baltic, separated from Russia by Lithuania and Poland. We played at an old communist union worker's hall, complete with about seventy-five burly union guys, 50-year-old stocky workers who could not believe their eyes. The show drew about 3,000 young folks, and they acted like we were the Beatles. They cheered, threw jewelry, and halfway through the set started throwing things at the union worker security guards. The old, thickset guys drifted into the crowd to throw some punches and, within seconds, large mass fights were taking place right during our song, "Kill the Light," probably our most nihilistic song.

I surveyed the scene, and it just popped into my head to sing "The Internationale." I guess I wanted to let all know that I had respect for the socialist values even though I represented punk rock from America. Within a few seconds, the place stopped, and you could've heard that proverbial pin drop. "In the cities and in the fields, the struggle carries on. The Internationale... unites... the world in song."

It really was something to see everyone frozen, staring at me, like, *"How does this American know 'the Internationale'?"* It was a beautiful sight. We then ripped into "Greedy and Pathetic." Dance-mad craziness ensued and the union guys stepped back. It was the most off-the-hook gig of the Russian tour.

After the show, our driver and handlers, Adam Schwartz and his gal friend Sofia, tried to herd us into the van for the long ride back to St. Petersburg and then on to that bumpy two-lane road back into Helsinki, Finland. But I spotted a map, and it seemed to make no sense to backtrack on Russian roads over a thousand miles to end up in Eastern Scandinavia. We were due to play in Ireland three days hence. I could see as the crow flies it was much easier to simply cross Poland, drive north into northern Germany, and then catch a ferry from Hamburg or Denmark.

I sent our ride, begrudgingly, back without us, and we partied with the promoter, drinking top-shelf vodka. The next morning he drove us 30 kilometers to the Russian border outpost, which led into Poland. We arrived, got out of the van with our luggage, walked up to the small guard post, and announced we were ready to leave Russia. The two guards barely spoke any English. I am glad we had an English-Russian dictionary because what I learned was, due to the types of visas we had, leaving the country was forbidden by any way other than the way we entered. FORBIDDEN! *ZAPRESHCHENO!*

I had to think fast. I asked if I could use the phone to call our agent. I went into the back of the guard booth, picked up the receiver, heard the weak dial tone, and hell, there was no agent to call.

I stood there holding the phone, and then something occurred to me. I stepped back out to the head guard and told him my agent told me there were special papers that the guard must have, and I was to pay $100 a person. So I laid out six $100 bills on the table. The guard started to say, "Nyet," but I could see him staring at the money on the table. Then he said something that we had to look up. Loosely translated, what he said was, "But of course."

In minutes, I signed what looked suspiciously like a train schedule, and we were on our way, walking with our instruments in hand across the border into Poland, our pockets heavy with near useless rubles.

None of our experiences in Russia would have happened if not for the advice of a dear friend. Upon hearing that the Russian ruble crashed and that our hosts were doubling the starter money from $5,000 to $10,000, I was uncertain whether to go or not. Tim Yohannan offered to loan us the money, but still I was unsure whether or not to do it. I turned to my very close, longtime friend, Ulla Kopycinski, to see if she thought we should go or not. She answered, "In this life, you usually regret what you don't do, as opposed to doing what you want to do." It was great advice. Sadly, in 2015, Ulla took her own life. She is in my dreams, and I miss her terribly... fucking terribly.

Chris Wilder, the brilliant guitarist on *Shades of Brown*, MDC's guitarist for the years 1992-94, is a wonderful sweet human being, and I love him pretty fat. He is honest, good natured, and a perfect gentleman. Erica Liss was also in that lineup for those same years. She is a very fabulous person herself. We all got along so well. Sadly, this lineup didn't go as far as it should have. Al had some real legal problems due to drugs, and things got fucked up between us. Drugs can get in the way. Whatever goes up can certainly come down.

Sleeping With The Enemy

I'm sure everyone has done it. Maybe women fall prey to it more than men. I'm not sure of that. This is not a big heavy, it just sometimes happens, especially if you meet someone attractive: the hormones kick in, you meet someone you don't know, but suddenly the combat boots are knocking.

In Austin, Texas in the late '70s, I had a set of lesbian friends. We all hung out at the Hollywood, a disco that catered to lesbian clientele. I guess I fit in so well because I felt I was one of them. They couldn't stand macho, chauvinistic straight men and deep down, neither could I. These were the same women who took me to my first and only Runaways show (who were playing with the Ramones), where I participated in pogoing for the first time.

So, one night, I was with the girls and they introduced me to a friend. We seemed to have certain things in common and she seemed to really like me so we went to bed. I licked miles and miles of vagina, did every position I was capable of, smiled, and laughed and giggled. Later we talked about who we were and what we were about, and that's when it came out. I told her I was starting a punk band, hated the system, and hung out with lesbians on purpose.

She said she was vice president of the Young Republicans Chapter on the University of Texas campus. I was like, "Naw, no way," but I was soon to hear, "Sorry, but, yes." We started talking politics and discovered we disagreed on about everything under the sun except hanging out with lesbians in discos. Almost like garlic to a vampire, I was repelled. I grabbed my stuff and ran for the hills. She was nice, attractive, and, gosh, I am pretty much smitten by anyone who thinks holding my hand and hugging me tight is a good thing. Still, I ran for the hills.

The next time was almost a mirror occurrence. Once again I was with the girl gang and, at a certain point, one friend of a friend and I were there checking each other out. She was attractive to me, and me to her, so we were off to her place. Almost the same thing occurred: after the lovemaking comes the chitchat. Her uncles, I learned, were head honchos in the Ku Klux Klan. The Klan, according to her, helped people and looked out for the community. I asked her about burning crosses and all the vile racism. She acted like that was a long time ago and was way overblown and not at all what is going on with the Klan today. I was soon looking for my socks and again heading for the hills. Maybe I should have talked it out more, but I couldn't do it. Now, hopefully, I would be better at communicating; I'd like to think so. Hell, maybe not.

The last time happened in Chicago around 1988 with a friend's friend. I was staying with Motor, a friend of Eric from the band Life Sentence. His girlfriend had a friend with her, and she was very nice to me the whole night. MDC did its set, and we were heading back to Motor's. I found her looking at me with dreamy eyes, and by the end of the night we were together making the whoopee. It felt so right, all the pillow talk was warm and cool. And, looking back, all I can say is God bless being young. We just kept going and going. Of course, the next morning you start chatting, and that's when she shared with me that she was going back to the compound.

"What kind of a compound?" I asked.

"Oh," she said nonchalantly, "a white power compound sworn to prevent niggers from getting any more rights." She was against race-mixing and, all of a sudden, the volume went out. I could see her beautiful warm red mouth talking, but the volume was gone. This time my chest seemed heavy and I had trouble rising. I told her I disagreed with her but I didn't want to discuss it. I searched for my shoes, got them on, and ran.

These people didn't hurt me, and even my dear mother voted for Ronald Reagan, but I just couldn't hang with it. I didn't try to turn any of these experiences into learning moments. In each case, I just ran, which is too bad. For all of you, I wish all your love mates not be white supremacists.

Useless Pieces of Shit

I moved to Portland, Oregon in the summer of 1995, my escape from San Francisco. I had become quite the tweaker in 1993 and 1994. Drugs had played a big part in the 1970s punk scene. They were omnipresent, part of the background, the set dressing. They were just *there*. I'm sure most everyone's heard the stories about water from the CBGB's basement toilet being used to mix drugs to shoot up. The "No Future" ethos played into all our actions. No one thought about where they might be five or ten years from now. With Cold War hysteria turned up to ten, the specter of nuclear warfare was never far from our minds.

Anyway, obviously, I did my share of drugs. I never considered not doing drugs until I encountered the straight edge scenes of DC and Boston. Straight edge jibed well with our hardcore philosophy. As a political band, we felt we needed to be alert and clean. This worked out for me in the early '80s when I lived with my girlfriend Jenny Jo and helped raise the children. I quit drugs through mid 1986 when we were living together as a family. After we broke up sadly through a mutual decision, due to my being in a band and unwilling to make a long-term personal commitment, she left San Francisco for Northern California.

Even though I would go visit the kids every three or four weeks, I had a large emotional gap in my life as well as more spare time on my hands. Unfortunately, this gap and spare time was easily filled with drugs, in particular methamphetamine.

I was into the strong glass speed they had back then in the Bay Area. Hallucinations and such could keep one tweaked for eons, but it felt so warm. It was like speed cut with ecstasy. I got lost in many, many shadows during the tweak world of early '90s San Francisco. I was on the edge; I was really out there but didn't even realize it.

One night in late 1994, I did a gig out of my mind on speed. I had Val Kilmer/Jim Morrison visions. It was like being on a high-speed train going off the rails, and all of MDC was along for the ride, until the wreck came. I was a train wreck. San Francisco was getting hot for me with the police. Al was hot from dealing, and I was in the band whose name they hated. Anyway, I got scooped up at Alschvitz's on a raid, and he got busted for a third time. I went to court with Al as a witness for him, and the police and prosecutors stared hard at me. Al accepted a plea bargain and I realized that my days in San Francisco were numbered.

I was being a smarty-pants but really was heading for a big fall. I knew I had to get out, and for once in my life, I did. My friend, Heather Phillips, really helped me out. We did the *Man With the Golden Arm* reenactment: she chained me to the bed, and we got me clean. Within two weeks, we were headed to Portland where my son, Jesse, and stepdaughters, Rosel and Deidra, lived. We were setting out to make a new good life: a meth-free life.

Well, we arrived in my new hometown in the summer of '95, made some new friends, met good old Brian Payne, and my neighbor, Wheeler Carson. I heard Tom Roberts, a.k.a. "Pig Champion," was around, and I wanted to hook up. I got hired working as a teacher's assistant, which was challenging, if underpaid, work. By fall, we all needed to earn some extra money, and we started working five-hour, weekday swing shifts from 5 p.m. to 10 p.m. for UPS. So, we worked at the Portland airport (PDX) UPS hub. It was Heather and I, Wheeler, his gal, Susie, and my friend, Brian Payne, night after night, trying to memorize thirty ZIP codes and put the envelope in the right slot. It was okay.

The supervisor there barked at everybody, but that was par for the course. Always tagging along with him and doing his bidding was this guy who had no title, and rumor had it he had been there for ten years and never got a promotion. He would yell at people, then talk loudly, giving a pep talk that that made no one peppy.

One of the big no-no's on the floor at the UPS hub was eating at your post. Two girls got caught by the supervisor eating potato chips and were fired on the spot. One of the girls cried. The shift workers were hissing and booing under their breaths, but off we went back to work.

Wheeler grew his own pot, and he ate pot cookies nonstop. I couldn't begin to keep up. Half a cookie was good for me, but he ate them one after another, all day long, and all evening long. I was amazed. Wheeler would eat those cookies right at his station with the bag half-hidden, but not all that out of sight. Wheeler offered me one, and I took it and broke it in half.

Well, who is spying on us but the little rat-faced lackey? He came over, started shrieking at us, and grabbed the bag of cookies. He ran off with the bag to look for the supervisor, and I was forlorn, but finished my cookie. So, we were just frozen... what should we do? Wheeler just kind of shrugged, grinned and said, "Let's wait to get fired." I waited for the supervisor to come back and fire us. Ten minutes went by, then twenty, and then we heard a commotion at the end of the building.

An ambulance pulled up and both the supervisor and his lackey were brought out to sit in the ambulance. They were breathing heavy as they spoke to the EMT guys. Wheeler looked at me, and I said, "Let's just split," and the four of us walked out of the building past the guards and out to the cars. We never heard a word about it but, happily, our last checks did come in the mail two weeks later.

Still clean, not doing speed, I taught at an elementary school in deep southeast Portland in the mid 1990s, the neighborhood where I still live. It's gotten a lot better, but back then our neighborhood was a sad, white trash world mix of Pentecostals and meth-heads and poor folk. Thirty-three kids in the classroom, and some get sent to school with no coat in the winter, with no socks, hungry, without lunch money, with toothaches, colds, and assorted bruises.

I kept a bottle of Bactine handy for the nicks and scrapes and Ritz crackers for the hungry to munch on. The kids, considering what they were up against, were indomitably spirited. We played football and kickball during lunch, all the boys and three girls played, and inside everyone played chess. The kids liked chess. I pushed them to learn chess. These kids in this 'hood, nicknamed "Felony Flats," didn't have much. They had themselves and a few good adults, if they were lucky.

At the school, I listened, stayed positive, and insisted we were all in this together. On Parents' Day, a few people came. Two parents out of my 33 kids were in prison. We had a "Welcome Home from Prison" party in my classroom. It was a nice time, but the future loomed. One common Special Education teacher remark was "the apple doesn't fall far from the tree."

Drug Abuse Resistance Education, or DARE, is a group of police or police proxies who come into elementary schools and show off vehicles that they have repossessed from drug dealers and warn kids of drugs' dangers, and to look for drug behaviors that family members might exhibit. In the two times I participated, the DARE people exhibited a range of attitudes that varied from "deep concern to get Mom or Dad some help," to "It's time to get these drug addicts off the streets; be damned if it's your older brother or Grandma!"

School was chaotic when the DARE police officers were around. The cops loved to brag about cars they stole from drug dealers when they were arrested. Ah, but isn't stealing wrong? Maybe they do help some people, but I don't know when all the effort is put into arrest and incarceration and so little into rehab and recovery. DARE claimed marijuana was the gateway drug and told extreme tales of smoking pot one month and becoming a stone-cold killer addict the next. The stories were way too much and caused real confusion with the kids.

The last time the DARE officers visited with their dog and pony show, they journeyed heavily into the evils of pot and stated outright that it leads to meth or heroin. The kids were bewildered and started arguing, calling each other names, and saying such and such's mother is a pothead. At this point, the cops said it was time for them to leave, and that I should talk with the kids to see if they have some information, and they'll meet back with me in thirty minutes.

The topic was whether or not marijuana can kill you, and the kids all wanted to hear from Dave. "So can marijuana kill you, Dave?" the kids all wanted to know, to which I replied, "The only way marijuana can kill you is if a policeman catches you with it and beats you to death with his nightstick." It was almost as if I waited my whole life to say that. Silence filled the air along with the satisfaction that they were hearing the truth from someone they could trust.

I had been in Portland about ten months. Heather, my gal friend of two years, was offered a good job in Reno. I was finally in my son's hometown, and I liked my job as a TA, and it liked me as well. It was a tough decision, but I promised that I would follow her to Reno if her job panned out. After many tears, she got on the plane, and I thought, *I'm never going to Reno.*

After being clean for ten months, my li'l drug addict mind was at full greediness. I had gotten clean but without any support system or any realization of the level of my addiction. I wasn't doing hardly any drugs, but I was planning to. Lie to a girlfriend who saved your life and send her on her way so you can be free to do all the drugs you want... Two different people were on my shoulder talking to me: Good Dave and Bad Dave. Bad Dave was winning. Bad Dave won.

Within two weeks of Heather's departure, I got my way to be free to do drugs, gave up my apartment, and moved into Tom Roberts' (Pig Champion's) little room. This room was at Suburbia, a gig spot and practice hall. I had bumped into Tom at Rochelle Menashe and Joe "Go" Strum's apartment when they had just opened Suburbia. There are many stories about Suburbia. Tom was the janitor, and I became the assistant janitor. Tom had just got some fat royalty money from the movie *The Crow* for Pantera's cover of Poison Idea's song "The Badge."

At this point, I had escaped my methamphetamine use, the SF police and the entire SF speed world I had become a part of, thanks to

Heather Phillips. I put in a year doing teacher assistant work in Portland and after that year I assembled an MDC line-up with Eric Calhoun on guitar, Roby Williams on drums, Joe Strum (RIP) on bass, and myself. We recorded a 7-inch, "Pig Champion," with Tom Roberts for Honest Don's records, Fat Mike of NOFX's secondary label. Listen to Pig's wall of sound on that recording. I find it classic.

The summer of 1996, we did a show at La Luna in Portland with Ice T's Body Count, and Ice T called me "the original cop killer." Soon after, I booked a trans-Canadian tour that dropped down into the US on the East Coast and back across the states, home to Portland. I was almost a year clean and doing it out of sheer will power: no NA or rehab.

On the Canadian leg of the tour, we played these rundown hotel/tavern watering holes. In Vancouver, it was The Niagra; in Calgary it was The Calgarian. In London, Ontario, it was The York. All these places were worn-out establishments that seemed 75 years old or more. None seemed to have been refurbished. They sold 25-cent or 50-cent drafts. You got many down-and-outers just clinging to their beers all day.

At the Calgarian, we'd start out with our usual set, and the crowd would jeer us mercilessly until we caved and wound up singing Johnny Cash, Hank Williams, and other country songs. These places were a hoot, and sadly most of them are long gone now.

One night, we were playing The York in London, Ontario. More working women than usual were doing their thing and taking men into the rooms next to ours. They were rather worn-out looking types, not at the top of their game, but hey, who was I to judge? I was nursing my clean-from-drugs thing, "bare knuckling" as they say, making it but wondering for how long.

After our set, I left the bar to go up to the room. The band was downstairs where we played. We had been given separate rooms, and I was just kicking it, looking at the torn wallpaper. After a few minutes, I heard shouting and a loud ruckus. I rushed to the door and saw the Canadian London police chasing women up and down the hallway and in and out of the rooms.

As I turned the other way, a young blonde woman flew in through the door and slammed it shut behind us. I asked her what was up, and she put her finger to her lips for me to shush. She whispered, "If the police catch me, I'm gonna do time, for sure."

I followed her lead, leaned my back to the door, slouched to the floor, and listened. She went into telling me her life story.

She grew up dirt poor and hard in a broken family. She was in love once with a guy that got her into this, and now she was a full-on crack addict. The guy was long gone, and her life was an endless reality of "suck dick for crack." She looked like a damaged Barbie doll. Tall, with blonde hair, blue eyes, but with bad teeth and the hunted look of having been slapped around. She told me I had just saved her ass, and she was so grateful but wanted to know what the fuck an American was doing in a joint like this. I told her I was in the punk band that played downstairs earlier. She took my hand into hers and leaned into me as I put my arm around her. Within a few minutes, the commotion seemed to have ended, and the cops were gone with the women they must have arrested.

At this point, my Barbie friend took a pipe out of her pocket and loaded it with crack cocaine from an aluminum foil bindle. She took a long hit and held her breath the way one would with a hit of crack cocaine. The pipe was held out to me and she lit the lighter. I paused for a second and then took a long deep hit. My mind exploded… we lay there taking hit after hit as I held her while she cried and laughed. We kissed and held each other's faces. After thirty minutes or so, she passed out in my arms, and I dragged pillows and a blanket off the bed and made us as comfortable as possible before I passed out next to her, arms wrapped around one another.

I woke up the next morning. She was gone. On the floor was my open wallet. I had $200 in it but she'd taken only $40 of it and left this note, "Take care of yourself and I'll see you around, American punk rocker." I knew I would never see her ever again.

It kicked off another three-year drug run before I got clean for good in 1999.

Back in Portland, hanging with Tom Roberts was fun, especially spending his money on drugs. Portland used to, and maybe still does, have phone numbers you can use to call a dealer. Then a delivery guy would show up with dimes and twenties of cocaine and heroin in a car outside your house. We were doing oodles of drugs... I got my addiction back fast.

We started working on songs, and we came up with the concept and songs for The Submissives, female-domination inspired lyrics put to punk and hardcore. It came together fast and effortlessly. Tom bought Metallica and Stiff Little Fingers albums, and he bent the riffs and repurposed the rhythms. Watching Tom work was a pleasure. We conjured songs like "Lesbian Biker's Clubhouse Slut" and "Submissive For Your Love," which just rolled out of our mouths and guitars. We reached a pinnacle of drug inspired and induced creativity.

In two weeks, we devised fourteen songs. We shopped it to Fat Mike of Fat Wreck Chords, and he generously backed it. Mike sent us a lot of cash, and the album was put out on the Honest Don's label. I was tweaking my brains out again, with a bankroll to sustain it.

The Submissives drummer was a sweet man, Steve Andrews, who did no drugs. He was a bit freaked out by our drug abuse, and it alienated him from us. The band lasted about four months in all. We managed a couple shows but ultimately the weight of Tom's and my drug addictions made even a band practice too hard to accomplish. We unraveled and didn't bother to try any more.

Tom Roberts died from heart failure in early 2006. He is what they use the word "legend" for: the way he toured, and practiced, and lived. He had the aura of Orson Welles, a deep voice, and a complete presence. He played guitar just like a-ringin' a bell. I loved Tom, miss him, and wish we could write another song together. Rest in Peace, dear Tom "Pig Champion" Roberts.

Not Just Falling Off the Wagon But Under It

I had a few bad drug years in my life but 1997 and '98 were the worst. I'd gotten myself whacked out pretty good with Tom Roberts on meth but after I went through my Submissives' money, I turned to working in the drug trade. I became a beard for my methamphetamine-dealer friend. This involved driving him around to pick up large batches of speed, four ounces at a time, breaking it into smaller units, and redelivering it to his customers. My dealer-friend had warrants out for his arrest and I had a clean record; thus, I was the beard doing the driving and using my clean truck.

One day, my dealer pal traded some speed for a Mazda Miata and couldn't resist driving it around. The plates that he'd been told were clean ended up not being so clean. He was pulled over and after a high-speed chase, he was arrested for resisting arrest. He had piled up legal matters so he faced a decade in prison. This left me his business and I jumped into it. It was my turn to hold the bag and I really took to it quickly. I cooked a little speed but basically distributed it. I dragged a few very nice people through my sludge, like my girlfriend at the time, Debbey, and her best friend, Becky, two of the nicest people you might ever meet. Let me say here, sorry, to you two again.

Holy smokes, the stuff is addictive. I was consuming a lot, holding the bag as they say, and got busted. I didn't believe it at the time but getting busted took me off the merry-go-round. In the end, the police caught me with a relatively small amount but they did seem to have a certified reliable informant ready to testify to my much bigger activities. Within a month of getting busted I went into rehab voluntarily to show the sentencing judge that I was trying to rehabilitate myself and demonstrate to the court that I was being pro-active about getting past my drug problem.

I was wise to hold out on the DA's first deals of fourteen and then nine months, and basically got a four-month reduced sentence at the Restitution Center for work release where I got to work, save money, and complete a long rehab.

I have been sixteen years clean as of this writing, and I am so glad I have been. Drug and alcohol addictions are tough to beat. It's physical and mental, and it involves psychology and emotional well-being that you were either given and had ingrained in you as a child or not. I am blessed to have been able to make that choice and back my way out of addiction. In NA/AA they say, "There but for the grace of God goes I." I am very fortunate to have made my way back to clean and good living when many others have not. I say a prayer for those who are stuck.

At about that time, I took over fulltime parenting responsibilities for my son, Jesse, from Jenny Jo. Things had gotten complicated in Jenny Jo's personal life, and she asked me to take care of Jesse, who was 12 years old. Deena Wallace, my son's friend, helped me out a lot and gave me a place to stay until I was able to transfer my probation. My mom and dad made an offer for me to come home to Glen Cove with my son. I took that opportunity and I am really glad I did. The ghosts and triggers of my speed use were very heavy so the possibility of relapse was a real danger in Portland at the time. My son and I headed to Long Island.

Just like that, we were East Coasters. In 1998 and 1999, MDC did nothing for the first time since the band started. I parked cars in New York City and eventually got back to being a teacher's assistant before returning to school to earn a Masters degree in Education for teaching Special Education.

A lot of people helped me in that period, and I am thankful to all of them: parents, family, friends, and counselors. I hurt and let down people, and I have tried to make amends. If you are one I have left out, forgive me, contact me and let me try. I am far from a perfect person, but I am trying to get my shit straight and please help me continue to do that.

After moving back to New York to live clean and sober with my parents, I had to start re-teaching myself how to live. This was a slow process. For the first few years, I was not comfortable in my own skin. I could go through the motions, but I felt everything... just seemed off. As far as trying to feel sexual or even attempting some kind of intimacy, I felt rather numb. I started wondering, *Is this it?*

Without my dependence on drugs, I had to relearn how to become loose, spontaneous, and easygoing, so I could find the path to good places and celebrate life. I had to free myself to make those connections and break through depressive modes and addictive behaviors. I had some bumpy times in New York: losing my teaching job and my lover of two years in Portland, doing some Oregon county time on account of drug dealing, and worse, learning how to live without meth. In New York, I was still on probation.

The newest challenge was dealing with some gnarly tooth pain. Methamphetamine is not good for your teeth. Sure, sure, this sounds trite, but please let me share with you. Please don't just brush your teeth but floss as well. If you like your teeth, don't do speed. Now I know there is something groovy about body odor and being crusty. I used to love to wear a pair of jeans until they could almost stand up on their own, but there is nothing groovy about toothaches, and the only way not to have them is through dental hygiene. Blah, blah, sounds boring, right? I was about to have my fifth root canal in three years. I had two ultrasound teeth cleanings and a periodontal gum cleaning: a root planing and scaling. Three crowns were installed as well. It wasn't cheap, and it wasn't painless.

I've had a weird assortment of dentists through the years, starting with Dr. W, the one from childhood. He was an ex-Air Force dentist who filled my mouth with gigantic silver fillings that are infamous for cracking the tooth twenty years down the line when your teeth get brittle. He labeled me the "juicy kind" at the tender age of eleven because of being a drooler. I endured all his pro-America rhetoric during the Vietnam War and once on gas I tripped-out that he was plotting against me. Later I learned that it wasn't me per se. He was having a long-term affair with his nurse before his subsequent divorce from his wife. I knew there was a plot going on; it just didn't really concern me. It did, however, make me lose my ability to truly enjoy Nitrous Oxide, or laughing gas. Since then, I have remained a strict Novocain absolutist.

I had a dentist in Chinatown, San Francisco, with attractive cut-rate prices. I called Dr. K, said I had $300, a lot of dental problems, and he urged me, "Come on down, we take good care you." He gave me a root canal, two fillings, and a deep cleaning before the big tour I was about to go on. It scared me when he had to climb up on a stool to get over and into my mouth.

After that, I found a fabulous gay dentist named Dr. D, who was a lovely man and his oft told remark to me was, "Straight men sure gag easy." I always tried to assure him I was bi, but he could see through me. He was very pleasant, and I loved his décor, his wit, and particularly his affection for Divine. He was one of the many dentists to chide me to floss or lose my teeth.

Then, in Portland, I had a string of foreign dentists: one from Iran, one from Lebanon, one from Russia. I guess it was because I started using mall dental clinics. I was always more comfortable with them than those rooted in the community, family practitioner types that might question my amphetamine-enriched skin tone and the sunken eye look I had developed with my druggie lifestyle of the past five years.

Back on Long Island, my mouth pulsing like a cartoon goose egg, I was in need of a yet another dentist. My teeth were sensitive to everything hot, cold, and in-between. They were doing this 48-hour throb thing, *ouch!* I decided to give the phone book a good look. Low and behold I found a woman dentist, a Dr. Louisa. *What a poetic name,*

I thought to myself as the pain intensified, blurring her name and number on the yellow page. I reached out and called, got through, and the next day she could take me in. Her office was right next to the local high school of this prominent North Shore, Long Island community. I worked nearby. I was reminded of this when noticing the three teenage girls in the waiting room with their mothers. The art on the walls and the magazine selection all had a very strong female theme going on, which is nice enough, and, hey, I'm all pro girl, girls rock... you know what I mean.

So I get in there, and we meet. She was about 35-40 years old, very attractive with the most engaging Mona Lisa-like smile. I hit it off with her, and we talked about music, art, museums, high school kids these days, about root canals, getting a place to live, theater, radio programming, and whether my Novocain was kicking in or not. We proceeded to spend the next forty minutes together cleaning out the rotted part of my tooth and setting me up with a temporary filling. My mouth felt so much better, and what's more I felt safe and in good hands. We said goodbye and made arrangements for me to return in four days.

Those next days went by swiftly, and I returned. This time no one was in the waiting room, and the doctor's assistant was there. She greeted me and motioned me into the inner office and to the chair.

"My name is Kirsten, Louisa will be right with you," she cheerfully informed me. She was young, bright, very sassy, with short bangs in a Dutch boy cut and very clean white teeth. The good doctor joined us, asked me how I was doing, and got right to work hitting my gum up with a big shot of Novocain as I laid back and got comfortable. She got over me poking around, pulling out the temporary filling, drilling a little here and a little there, leaning into me, pushing against me. I was aware of her breasts pressing into my shoulder and arm. I could feel her breath, hot, and smell the antiseptic scent of mouthwash. Her perfume washed dizzily over me, and she smelled really good. I enjoyed the rapport she shared with her assistant. It was confident and engaged in that professional way we patients depend on. Yet, at the same time, it felt intimate, and I felt I was let in on that intimacy.

I knew this was dentistry, and that they were professionals, and I was but one of many patients they see daily, but between the haziness that comes with Novocain, the short sharp jolts of pain, the chemistry between the mysterious dentist and her sassy assistant (are they lovers or aren't they?), I started to melt, and feel an instantaneous affinity toward these women. I felt quite safe and powerless, flat on my back, mouth wide open, in the hands of these women. Well, how do I put this? I got aroused. And with that male arousal comes that, ah, what is the right word? An erection. I tried to think about baseball, about jail, about everything non-arousing I could come up with, all to no avail. There I lay with my mouth wide open. I had fronted myself off to these women as a truly unique sort of person, but now, maybe I was more like a weird, gosh, let's get rid of him quick kind of person. I tried to express apologies with my eyes. Remember, my mouth is wide open. Dr. Louisa smiled and chuckled, and Kirsten giggled. I was so glad neither was repulsed.

"Well, well, let's give Dave a chance to relax a second." That they did, and momentarily returned to finish off building up the tooth and complete the new filling. I was abhorred by my traitorous blood flow, but Dr. Louisa looked at me, and said, "I've been complimented on my dental work, but never quite like this. Let's get you back in here for a teeth cleaning in about two weeks, and I really recommend you get your teeth cleaned every three months. Okay, Dave?"

She looked so beautiful and strong and vital. I was intrigued, and let me tell you, my heart was pounding. So, afterwards, I went shopping and bought a lavender silk shirt. I clipped my nails pretty and bought a subtly pleasant cologne all in an effort to let myself be free to make those connections and break through the depressive modes and addictive behaviors.

Back to School

From 2000 to 2003, still living in Glen Cove, I got my master's degree in Special Education from Long Island University, and I taught a class of fairly high functioning developmentally delayed or disabled kids at a school in New York City. I used to work in a regular class with special needs kids, helping to "mainstream" them, as it's called. As water flows down hill, I got pushed to where the need was greatest. And the need for teachers who work with the developmentally disabled was the greatest need.

I learned to appreciate the job. No administrators got in my face to get me to teach to the test. I taught my kids reading, weather, and math skills (mostly how to tell time and make change) all in the manner I desired. We talked recycling, map reading, and we did a little history and geography. I worked it out with my kids so that when the principal came into the room, we'd go through a drill.

I'd ask, "Who freed the slaves?"

They knew to collectively answer in their own big eyed, little way, "Abraham Lincoln."

"Jamal, what happened to him?"

Jamal answered, "He got shot by a bad man."

"Thomas, who was Martin Luther King, Jr.?"

"He was a great man who fought for justice."

The principal would smile and wonder how I was doing this

and leave the class, and we wouldn't see him again for a week or two, sometimes for a month. Perfect.

Being developmentally disabled, or what used to call mentally retarded, was only part of the problem for most of my kids. They also possessed a mixed bag of emotional, processing, and physical disabilities. Two of my kids, Thomas and JP, also had autism. They were indifferent much of the time and had compulsive behaviors constantly being exhibited, so we tried to redirect them. For instance, JP would rock for hours at a time, unless you stopped him. Thomas had the habit of repeating everything you said. Let me add that Thomas had the highest IQ in the class, 66, but nevertheless he could monologue whole episodes of *The Simpsons*, and he memorized and sang whole sides of rap albums. He couldn't tell you the difference between "will run, now runs, and ran," – past, present, and future, tense that is – but he could recite the names of all Saturn's 22 moons and the weekend schedule of departing trains at Grand Central Station.

That's the failure of IQ tests. If you don't test well or relate to the questions, then you score poorly. In fact, one of my students, Dorothy, was very heads-up and very confident. She thought on her feet and was very street smart. I don't know what to make of the whole deal about intelligence. She couldn't do math or read so well, but she took a subway by herself from Brooklyn to her aunt's in the Bronx. I've had problems accomplishing that.

Jamal had been born 2.2 lbs, a fetal alcohol syndrome crack baby. His emotions were always high-strung. He freaked out at the drop of a hat. He heard voices, talked to himself, and felt persistently persecuted (just like a typical evangelical, except for them, it's not considered bad). Teaching him how to share, cope with disappointment and failed expectations, not to call out without raising his hand, and not to get angry when his answer was wrong, was a constant challenge. We were trying to teach him how to cope with his emotions. He was the biggest handful. But his successes were the most enjoyable.

Jamal frequently freaked out and threw tantrums. I had to usher the other children out of the room because he'd eventually attack one of them. I had to restrain him while he kicked, scrapped, scratched, screamed, and on and on, sometimes for 20 minutes, sometimes for two hours. He'd yell, "Shut up, you stupid fuck-o, shut up." He screamed "fuck-o" over and over again.

When Jamal was absent, it was like being at the beach. It was almost a holiday. He had so much vinegar; he questioned everything and was never passive. On many levels, he was a cool kid. He reminded me of a small angry punk rocker, my own little Sid Vicious. He scratched me and spit on me dozens of times.

In front of the class and the African-American teachers' assistant, Gertrude, who worked in my classroom, he asked me, "How come you're not brown like us?"

Gertrude and the entire class looked at me, and I calmly replied, "I am brown, but just a lighter shade of brown. Human life started in Africa; my people left a little earlier, but I feel we are all brown here."

Gertrude smiled, and the kids all looked satisfied by the answer. Month in month out, my class and I got tighter and tighter.

The few days I had to call in sick, all hell broke loose. Jamal would go into hysterics. No work could get done. I had to plan out my missed days very well. I told them in advance, wrote on the calendar, reminded them and assured them I'd be back. My school had terrible trouble getting substitutes, and they kept bringing back this rotten, power tripping, old man in his late sixties, Mr. Buck. He was hard of hearing and got into power struggles with my kids. When he started to lose the fight, he resorted to dirty tactics: name calling and holding grudges.

The last time Mr. Buck subbed for me he had a very rough day. I tried to coach him how to stay calm, redirect the tension, stay above the fray, and all the classic teachers' mantra stuff. Of course, he didn't listen and lost it.

On my desk the next morning, I found a letter he had left for me to read. He wrote that Jamal started challenging him, wouldn't follow directions, and then got all the kids involved calling him Mr. Bucko, not Mr. Buck, and he didn't like it. I read the blow by blow account of his day, shook my head imagining all this, and then chuckled as I realized the kids weren't calling him Mr. Bucko, they were calling him Mr. Fuck-o.

Being at my parents' house with my son and getting away from Portland was pleasant. Once you're busted, the police in Portland never seem to leave you alone. More than once, the police pulled me out of my car, and I was told to lie on the ground as they illegally searched it. It was good to be around my parents as well. For over twenty-five years I lived in Austin, San Francisco, and Portland, rarely seeing them for more than a few days here and there. I was far away from any remnants of my band, though, and that was unfortunate.

I was writing a column for *Maximum Rocknroll* magazine when I was living on Long Island, and one day in my inbox was a letter from a Matt Van Cura from Port Jefferson, Long Island, a young bass player who wanted to get together and jam. I knew a drummer, John Soldo from the Skatalites, and he had a guitar buddy named David Hahn from the ska band Mephiskapheles and an entity known as Dub Is My Weapon. The four of us got together and sounded really good fast.

Before long, we had most of the first album and various songs from different MDC eras worked out. We were practicing in Hicksville, Long Island when a booker from CBGB walked by, heard us, and offered us a gig as MDC. Soon, we were working it up and down the coast with Molotov Cocktail, and played a short tour with Ratos de Porão from Brazil, and another short tour with the DC band, the Goons.

My son, Jesse, got along well with his grandparents. It was really wonderful to see their relationship develop, and this allowed me the freedom to return to what I do best: playing music and going on tour.

Millions of Dead Cowboys

Ratos de Porão suggested we come down to Brazil, so by summer 2001, we headed down and had a little tour worked out starting in Sao Paulo, then down to Curitiba, Pirenópolis, and Porto Alegre, then back up into the suburbs of the 22 million-thronged city of Sao Paulo, escorted by the wonderful Flav San. It was incredible, and we played with Olho Seco, a classic old punk band from the 1980s. Brazil was, and is, so different from anything I'd ever seen. It was lush, tropical, and teemed with luscious fruits. Living was easy if you were an American on a small stipend. The shades of green seemed almost prehistoric, while the wildlife was alluring. Brazil was a crazy place to play with large frenzied crowds in love with the music.

By 2002, Dave and John had moved on, but Matt and I soon found replacements. Brendan Beckawies of Piglet and Stockyard Stoics was on guitar, and on drums was Albatross Basin from Ludichrist and The Plungers. Two Japanese women played in the Plungers, and through them I learned a whole colony of Japanese punks lived in NYC with bands playing out all over. CBGB was going off with all kinds of festivals and gigs; meanwhile, Sturgeon from Choking Victim and Leftover Crack was living in the infamous C Squat and throwing free outdoor Tompkins Square Park events. NYC was thriving in the 2000s, and the East Coast offered quite a lot of cool gigs. Rebellion Festival from England did some East Coast events with the Addicts and Angelic Upstarts at Asbury Park.

This version of MDC with Brendan and Albatross toured down to Florida and flew out to the West Coast, reconnecting with the late great Showcase Theatre in Corona, California. We gigged throughout the San Francisco Bay Area, Sacramento, Fresno, Santa Cruz, and toured Europe in 2001 with Molotov Cocktail. The next year we played the MAD "With Full Force" Festival in the former East Germany, where we played with Motorhead, the Distillers, DRI, and Agnostic Front for crowds of 20,000 people. In the UK, Darren's Rebellion Fest has been going on for years, first as Holidays in the Sun, then it morphed into Rebellion Fest, mostly held in Blackpool, north of Liverpool. These annual fests feature fifty to sixty bands, with everybody from Rancid and Cock Sparrer, to the Subhumans, the Business, and Crass joining in. It really is something to see, and you do see punks and skins just hanging out with no problems.

In 2003, Ron Posner expressed interest in returning for a tour, so Matt, Ron, and percussion ace, Mike Pride, and I did a European tour with Dynamite Club. Ron had been living back in Venezuela, looking after his aging mother, after leaving the Bay Area in the '90s. Needless to say, it was great to have Ron back, and we pulled off an explosive European tour. After the tour, Mikey Donaldson came back to us on bass, and we recorded our *Magnus Dominus Corpus* album at Coney Island Studios with the talented Don Fury.

MDC

Magnus
Dominus
Corpus

CORPSES
OF THE ULTIMATE
DOMINATORS

Back Out to Portland, 2004 - Present

In 2003, Jesse had graduated high school and moved back to Portland to live with friends. After the 2003 European tour ended, I met a woman named Eva and stayed in Vienna; these were some of the best days of my life. We then traveled together to India. After being in India for a month, I got a call from my brother saying, "Mom is in the hospital." She was more than in the hospital; she had had a brain aneurysm. She was on life support so I got myself back to Long Island for her wake and funeral. It was in 2004. My father was a wreck so I stayed with him for a few months, and then spoke with Jesse, who said he wanted to start Portland Community College. And so in the fall of 2004, I officially moved back to Portland.

Starting in 2005 through 2007, MDC had its original lineup. I booked us a DIY US tour via Facebook, and we played a lot of odd little corners of the country, such as Rockford, Illinois, and Dubuque, Iowa, and at little record stores. Al still had legal problems, so for our European tours, we met Dejan Podobnik, a Serbian living in Amsterdam who was playing with Ojos de Gatos. He plays, in his words, "brutal style" drums. We did long Euro tours in 2005 and '06.

MDC was back to playing from 90 to 120 gigs a year right up to 2012, when we slowed it down a touch. By 2008, we started playing with Mike Smith on bass here in America because Mikey Donaldson moved full time to Europe and had immigration issues going back and forth.

Mikey Donaldson played on half of MDC's first 1982 debut and on the *Magnus Dominus Corpus* album. Mike was very much a rare, prodigy style bassist. He really did shred speed metal before the term was coined and had an incredible melodic sense. He was a founding member of the Offenders, he played with DRI on some of their albums, with Tony of the Nitwits of the Netherlands, and on the Sister Double Happiness debut album, where his melodic sense can be heard in the slow bluesy bass lines.

At first, we were never that close. He wasn't a singer kind of guy. We traveled together well but his real bond was with Ron Posner. They liked to play together a lot.

Mikey loved Swedish hardcore and all things Swedish. He hooked up with a Swedish gal friend, Selina Hackennson, and loved to travel with her to obscure parts of Europe. She was our merch assistant along with Arno Ooms on many a tour. They were playful and fun to watch. Mike would mess with Ron by changing the meticulous order in which he lined items up out of his suitcase, such as changing where the pants and socks were laid out.

Fuck, we all have demons of one sort or another, and some people can get a hold of theirs, and there but for the grace of God goes I. Check out the bass playing on the Offenders' "Lost Causes" single. Check out the bass break in "My Family Is A Little Weird," the popping bass sound on the start of "John Wayne..."

Mike Donaldson was exceptional. He called me the day before he died. He was broke in Barcelona, Spain, and asked me for some money. I sent $100. He was dead 24 hours later. I don't know the circumstances, but I'm glad he knew he could call me and count on me to help out and send something. The world is stripped of a very special guy and musician. RIP Mikey Donaldson.

Mike Smith and I started playing out as MDC Acoustic, in which we play folksy sets of old and new songs. Around this time, in short order, he became my friend, roommate, bassist, and co-conspirator.

He is a gifted artist/muralist, a songwriter, and another talented bass player to have entered my life. He is the product of the Idaho public schools' music department. I feel I can share everything with him. We have cried in one another's arms and know in our darkest moments we can turn to each other.

Russ Kalita played second guitar and filled in for Ron when he couldn't get away from obligations he had in Venezuela. We played the Northwest extensively, up and down the coast, as well as doing national tours with Citizen Fish, the Restarts, Verbal Abuse, and Subhumans. We released two compilation EPs, the *Solid* EP with art by Dick Lucas of Citizen Fish. It featured our song "Maryjane for President" and included songs from Mouth Sewn Shut and Embrace the Kill, too. Then we released "Patriot Asshole" on the *Human* EP, with art by Kieran Plunkett. The single also included the Restarts, Phobia, and Embrace the Kill. In 2010, we recorded the *Mobocracy* split with the Restarts of the UK.

In 2010, I was considering moving permanently to the Big Island. My longterm relationship with Eva was falling apart and we wanted to try to save it. We tried repeatedly and much to our chagrin, it did not work out. We split up but I did become reaquainted with my love of the beach, the sound of the waves, the smell and feel of the mist. Hawaii is an enchanting place built upon volcanic rock.

In 2011, the band did an exciting tour with old friends, the British Subhumans. It was big fun with great crowds. But before and after the tour, I was with my brothers often and we took turns looking out for and taking care our father. He had a few terrible falls including one on my watch. Those that have done this kind of home care of a loved one know it's so tough. It is hard to see a parent losing his strength and memory.

At the end of December 2012, my father passed away at home. My brother Roger was in the house with him. Many people feel their parents are bigger than life and I am one of them. The world stood still for us. We were all relieved on one level, but devastated on another. We realized things would never be able to go back to the way we once were, and this is natural. We all face this at one time or another. I lived my life as if I was Peter Pan and those days are now behind me. I feel I finally became an adult. Well, maybe.

In 2013, we racked up over eighty gigs with new drummer Jesse Cobb of the band, Dirty Kid Discount, including heading off to Australia and New Zealand. Down under was long a dream come true. My father served in the Pacific during WWII and talked about New Zealand as a place he dreamed about going back to some day that never happened for him. We played four shows in Australia, flying around the country because the distances between cities are so long. We played Brisbane, Adelaide, Melbourne, and Sydney. People are so far away from us here in the US and Europe, in that part of the world. All our shows were well attended and people so friendly. We flew to Auckland, New Zealand for our last show and there our new drummer would meet his future wife, Tove Partington. This part of the world is a very enchanting place.

In 2014, we were having a slow year, so I went east to help my brothers pack up my mom and dad's house.

Love In Every Breath

In May 2014, I went east from Oregon to pack up my parents' house. They had both passed, and it was time. It was a few months earlier, however, when I fell down a flight of stairs in Hawaii. I was carrying a full five-gallon water cooler jug up the stairs when I missed a step. I came down those stairs hard on my shoulder, on my neck, and on my lower back. I laid there in agony but managed to slowly creak my way to my feet and walk it off. A night later, I was flying back to Portland and thought, *I'm a little stiff but okay.* Fast-forward ninety days, and there I was packing and lifting at Mom and Dad's. I guess with the stress of moving things and re-visiting a lot of emotional memories, it all started to wreak havoc upon me.

On the second night, my whole body just shut down. I could barely move and was in full-on "10 pain" mode – the crying face on the universal pain assessment chart – that was me. I went to the hospital. They looked me over, gave me a shot, and sent me home. I went back the next night, they gave me another shot, and they sent me home again. When the painkiller wore off, I was back in excruciating pain. The third night I was in such torment I begged to be admitted. At that point, they gave me a blood test and I was found to have a staph infection that was poisoning my whole system, including savaging my organs. Fevers were coming fast so I was a complete wreck.

Finally I was admitted into Glen Cove Hospital but it was

Thursday night of the Memorial Day weekend. They put me in a room. By this time, I was running a 102-degree fever, hallucinating, hearing voices, and seeing gremlins everywhere. I thought it was snowing in my hospital room. At this point, I could hear people talking but could not supply a coherent answer. They were talking about heroic measures and getting a health care proxy to make my health decisions. I was mostly worried about how all the snow was gonna pile up in my room.

My brother, Roger Hanlon, was trying to make sense of it all. Poor Roger dealt with two brothers and a father passing on him in the last couple of years. Helpless, he just said, "Hang in there, brother," as he did the next night, too. I felt I was slipping away – my reality, my ability to comprehend, and my life. But I wanted to get out of the hospital. *At least get me to the beach and I'll attempt to swim home to Portland. What the heck, become fish food,* I thought. I had talked to Mike Smith, my MDC acoustic partner, and to Ron Posner, my good buddy and long-term partner in MDC electric. They were telling me to hang tough, and I was, "Yeah, yeah," but still I was plotting to get to a taxi and make my way to the beach. Crazy and lost and fevered but ready for a long swim, I was a mess.

The next day, my relatively new friend and roommate from Portland, Rebekah Creswell, showed up. We had met six years before when MDC was playing a bar in Bend, Oregon. Rebekah and four of her friends couldn't get in because they were underage. Mike Smith and I went out with our acoustic guitars and played them a set acoustically. It was neat and cool, and they were sweet and appreciative, and I didn't think about it until we ran into each other in Portland one day.

I believe it was the first time she came over when I asked, "Why don't you build a loft in the living room and live with us?" We all laughed. Rebekah went home to the dorm at her nursing school. Then somehow this idea surfaced — having a trailer in the driveway with an electric cord run out of Mike's room. So we went with it. Soon thereafter, she showed up, moved a trailer into the driveway, and since then she has been a dynamo of energy for our house, like getting our organic magical garden yard together, raising chickens, and doing hard work. Anyway, Rebekah was there in my hospital room, which forced me to focus.

"I am here to get you home," she stated, and started going over the doctor's orders and checking on the nurses' actions, like what they had followed through on, and what they had not. To get everybody in shape, she communicated with the supervisor. She held my hand while I was still talking gibberish. Somewhere in there, the switch was pulled: I really wanted this so-called life. Rebekah, with her nursing school training, directed traffic and looked over me. Memorial Day weekend finally passed, and it seemed the regular crew were back on the job and a health team was gonna work on the staph infection in my bones and try to prevent my organs from shutting down.

I was somewhat lucid, yet still hallucinating. I thought my wonderful nurse's assistant, a woman named Maria, was the Virgin Mary, and imagined I was her son. I was in ecstasy when she washed my hair. I cried. I felt it was very religious, and I am glad I experienced it. After a few days, Rebekah had to leave but she had brought my son. I only have one child, Jesse Dictor. It was his turn to look after me, and he did a great job. He assured me I was getting better. He was certain. I wasn't certain, but it was good my son was. It is beautiful to be looked after by your child. It can be sad in terminal situations, I know, but it is still really beautiful.

Then I got transferred from a little hospital to a big hospital — Glen Cove Hospital to Long Island Jewish Hospital/Manhasset — and it had a different rhythm. I recommend something: if you're in a hospital, then get to know everyone you can, and communicate the best you can with them all. Dear folks, I had a cast of thousands, lots of doctors. Some so young and sweet, I felt as if I was back in high school with them. I was really put through it all: ultrasounds, MRIs, blood test after blood test, and six intravenous antibiotics sessions a day. Some women on the custodial staff were from India and Sri Lanka and looked in on me because they thought I looked like Jesus. I started to wave them into my room, to hang with them, learned where they were from, and blessed pictures of their children. I went out of my way to share time and conversation with everyone. I wanted everyone on my side.

And I was getting better daily. My body had been pretty frozen up

— I was unable to move due to my back, neck, and shoulder injuries — but finally my legs came back. Since the beginning, I could hobble to the bathroom on my own, but now I started walking the halls with my walker. Finally, I got the news: I tested negative for the staph infection. They wanted to see at least five straight days clean which, in the next four days, I did indeed accomplish! I am so grateful to all who played a part in my recovery, including the people who stayed in touch with me on Facebook and encouraged me to write this book. I was floating along getting a little better every day.

Eventually, the bureaucracy learned my health insurance (Go Obamacare!) only paid fifty percent of out-of-state charges, and I was rolled out to the sidewalk in a wheelchair. Mentally, I was ready, and a cab arrived to take me to my parents' former home. The cabbie was Jamaican.

We started talking, and I said, "From now on, only love will come out of my mouth and be on my breath."

He said, "Way to go, brother," in his mellifluous Jamaican accent.

This is where I am at now. I am filled with grateful feelings to be alive. MDC is still going, and we are a political hardcore band on a mission from God. Thank you.

In Memoriam
with love & gratitude

In the thick of WWII, a man served in the Navy's Construction Battalion in the Pacific theatre. While he was at work building an airstrip, two Japanese soldiers emerged from the forest. Between them, they carried a white flag. The enemy soldiers surrendered to the man and his three comrades working with him. The incident was radioed into headquarters, and headquarters said someone would be sent to pick up the prisoners. Two Marine Corps officers arrived, sized up the situation, and determined a plan of action. They decided too many Japanese POWs had already been captured, so they ordered the man and his fellow SeaBees to kill the Japanese soldiers.

"This is not what we're fighting this war for," the man said. He refused the order, as did his three mates.

Angered by such insubordination, the Marines drew their side arms as the SeaBees brought their rifles to bear. They were in a taut standoff. Since the Marines were outnumbered, the man radioed his Naval superiors. They all stood there, guns frozen on one another until Navy personnel arrived, relieved the Marines, and took the prisoners away to safety, alive.

Of all his war service, this was the man's proudest moment. Even the Purple Heart he earned for taking a bullet in the ass didn't compare. He never bothered to collect his medal. If he wasn't fighting to do the right thing, then what was he fighting for at all? The man who raised me knew he did the right thing.

He was a good person who didn't tolerate racism, sexism, or homophobia. He always insisted my brothers and I treat women with respect, and never bully or pick on those weaker or less fortunate than us. My respect grew even more when he told me that WWII story in 2012, just months before he passed.

The time I spent looking after him with my brothers could be painful and tedious, but I was glad to have shared in this memory with him. It gave me insight into the man who had helped raise me and shape who I became. I was granted a rare glimpse that helped me to see why I tick the way I do. When I became dangerously sick in what was almost my deathbed two short years later, I could hear my father's voice telling me to live well and be the best I can be.

My mother was born on Christmas in 1925. She was a Depression kid who worked hard for everything, and she loved me with a deep momma's love. I was cut from her cloth: New England Yankee-meets-Napoli, Italian immigrant/Brooklynite. She was part Liz Taylor, but she also had this Eleanor Roosevelt air about her. She was erudite, a writer who worked in the New York City newspaper world. She followed Soviet leader Khrushchev and President Eisenhower around on her beat at the United Nations, reported on New York City mayoral campaigns as well penning small stories, local hero profiles and "cat stuck up a tree" type stuff. She loved it all. She loved Manhattan and was raised by her father, Billy Bland, a circus man, and her mother, Rose Fracionne, who assisted her own father doing boot repair. My great-grandfather was an Italian immigrant who came to America as a teen in the 1890s and landed in Prospect Park, Brooklyn, across from Manhattan.

My mother, Evelyn, was easy on me and told me, "You can do anything." She explained things gently, was my biggest cheerleader, read me poetry, and took me to Broadway plays, museums, and the beach my entire childhood. She rarely yelled and never hit me. She would give me a look every so often if I said something that crossed her ethics, and would finally tell me to go to another room to think about what I said.

I got in trouble twice with the police, once at seventeen and once in my early forties, and she straightened out the police and probation officers both times, standing out in the driveway of her and my father's house. She read them the riot act and threw around the names of city, county, and state officials while asking for badge numbers and dialing up her attorney.

When I was a teenager, police had jacked me up and threatened me for having a pack of rolling papers outside an Allman Brothers concert at Nassau Coliseum. I wrote a letter and filed a formal complaint. The police threatened that I would regret filing the complaint against them, and my mother told them off straight away. It was beautiful to watch, and she didn't even ask what I was doing with the rolling papers. She had interviewed Louis Armstrong for the newspaper back in the day, and he wasn't shy about smoking pot through the whole interview. She was no one's dummy. She took me in after my drug dealing charges when I was arrested in my 40s, talked to me about addiction, and watched as I became a special education teacher. I am so glad we had those years right before she passed.

On February 4, 2004, I was traveling in India after living in Europe for six months when she died suddenly of a brain aneurism. I know most of us love our mothers but I feel the need to emphasize how fortunate I was to have her in my life and on my side.

Epilogue

Well, about two years ago I began this book. I wanted to say writing this has been eye-opening, sometimes hectic and confusing, and exciting to capture. Some of this I wrote in the hospital and at home while lying around with a Pic in my arm doing antibiotics for six weeks. I recycled, reshaped, and rewrote other material from *Maximum Rocknroll* columns I wrote from the 1990s through the early 2000s.

I want to tell you so much more about other people: the British Subhumans, Keith Morris, Kevin Seconds, Dave Rubinstein of Reagan Youth, Joe Keithly, Toxic Reasons, Disorder, Chaos UK, KGB, Butthole Surfers, Verbal Abuse, and Brandon Cruz. All are, or were (RIP), extremely talented people. Other folks from Texas and California, from our early years, as well as friends and mates in the ensuing years with whom we've shared interactions, also deserve more time and anecdotes. My punk history has been chock-full and rich. I am so lucky.

The last 35+ years constitutes an amazing cultural phenomenon that we each created and often continue to carry on. I, for one, believe punk rock will never die. You, dear reader, continue to be my fuel.

Punk, to me, amounts to an angst railing against the conformity of the status quo. I saw firsthand the ideals of the hippie world fail and turn against itself. They embraced the consumerism and commodification of music as an industry, which turned rock and roll into a machine and musicians into cogs in that machine. That was my impetus to break free from corporate culture and fully submerge myself in punk.

I'm always so happy to see those new crops of young kids who are looking to bust out from the norms shoved down their throats. Those kids give me hope, and I believe punk rock will never die as long as the kids find passion, cause, and voice.

Acknowledgments

Thanks to my ever-loving mother Evelyn Bland Hanlon and my father Joseph Bartholomew Hanlon, my brothers Billy Dictor, Roger, Ricky, and Robbie Hanlon and passed brothers Randy and Rusty Hanlon.

Much love always:
Tammy Lundy, Gary Floyd, Randy Turner, Tim Yohannan, Jello Biafra, Missy Zwigoff, and all the lineups of MDC: Ron Posner, Alschvitz, Franco Mares, Mikey Donaldson, Gordon Fraser, Eric Calhoun, Bill Collins, Matt Freeman, Chris Wilder, Erica Liss, Joe Strum, Roby Williams, Tom Roberts, Matt Van Cura, Brendon Bekowies, Al "Albatross" Basin, David Hahn, John Soldo, Mike Pride, Mike Smith, Jesse Cobb, Russ Kalita, Felix Griffin, and Dejan Podobnik.

Miss Louise, my TV kindergarten teacher. Musical actress Julie Andrews, and Howard Wortley, my high school music teacher. Also Karen Polk, Corin Dunne, Connie Brunner, Marianne Beatty, Gail Borling, Bonnie Heyman, Jim Brighton, Joseph Zito, Mark Dubicki, Dean Bogan, Fortlaroy Sullivan, Bradley Stone and Gary Prentiss.

My first vegetarian love Marilynn Hayes, kindred spirit Katherine Congdon, my precious Marla Bloch, Barbara Nightingale, Alice Loskot, Ginny Pretat, Gail Borling. To Patty Dubicki, what a childhood...
Thank you Jenny Jo Brown, my son Jesse Dictor, Jen's children Rosel, Deidra, and Bethy Chance Ward.

Thanks to friends and loved ones Fred Hofer, Ulla Kopicinski, Sabine Grosse, Candace Blankenship, Deena Wallace, Doreen Knaust, John The Baker, Sarah Heidler, Mara Beth Israel Ube, Jessica Norris, Erin Cookman, Kieran Plunkett, Christina Dubicki, Sweet Gwendolyn, Krissy Manchon, Kya Shayla, Kimmy Katt Hargrove, Stefan Zvokelj, Peter Vaughan Shaver/Sound Advice and Sergei Escarmis-Costa.

Friends that helped me with this book, like David Ensminger and Craig Williams, Robert Brokenmouth and Richard Ellis. To Stan Mueller and True Underground Network Publishing for his encouragement and book title. To Summer Halstead and Paul Cruikshank. To the fabulous and accomplished Jen Joseph, my final editor and publisher.

I want to thank all the punks worldwide who have supported us, who have supported our band by coming to see us live, buying our music, t-shirts, stickers and such. All the bands that were generous with us in any way. All the magazines big and small and other media people that cared to report about us. All the people that have put us up, fed us, nurtured us or helped get us down the road.

Thanks to all those of good spirit

Thank you, Mother Mary, (Isis) in the sky, our universal mother

Photo & Art Credits

pp 3: Stefan Zvokelj
pp 12, 24, 52, 66, 182, 191:
   courtesy of Dave Dictor
pp 10, 34, 39, 44, 58, 60, 73, 88, 90,
   91, 92, 98, 150,176, 188:
   courtesy of Ron Posner
pp 29: Tammy Lundy
pp 30: Ripper magazine
pp 36, 40, 56: Carlos Lowry
pp 47: Randy Turner
pp 48: cover: Ed Colver
pp 57: Buxf Parrot
pp 62: Tim Yohannon / Maximum Rocknroll
pp 85: Murray Bowles
pp 94: Lisa "Bat" Smith
pp 108: Vince Packard
pp 112: Murray Bowles
pp 116: Joe Britz
pp 120: John "Quill" Marquand
pp 123: photo/Mickey Scopt, layout/Alan Schultz
pp 126: courtesy of Gilman Street archives
pp 130: Winston Smith
pp 133: Ken Salerno
pp 140: Mark Tippin
pp 144: Candance Blankenship
pp 150, 192: Jenny Jo Brown
pp 171: Carlos Folorzano Smith
pp 172: Ilvy Maijen
pp 180: Matt Van Cura
pp 181: Mike Smith
pp 190: Lindsey Lutts McGuire

for additional MDC history, photographs, and more:
www.mdc-punk.com